CHRISTOLOGY

OF THE

FAMILY

CHRISTOLOGY

OF THE

FAMILY

STRAIGHT FROM A PASTOR'S HEART
SERIES - VOLUME I

REV. MICHAEL LESSARD

Kravitz & Sons
INNOVATORS IN PUBLISHING, MARKETING AND ADVERTISING

Kravitz and Sons LLC
1301 Farmville Blvd, Suite 104
Greenville, NC 27834

Published by Kravitz and Sons LLC.
ISBN: Softcover   979-8-89639-088-6
            eBook   979-8-89639-087-9

Library of Congress Control Number: 2025902802

CONTENTS

FOREWORD

The purpose of this book is to convey to you the primary ministry of the Church. The heart of the gospel is the pastoral care of the people of God. The message of the gospel is centered on the ministry of Jesus in healing the sick, reconciliation, and teaching. I hope to refocus our attention on the central elements of the Christian community.

The renewed awareness of the ministry of Jesus shifts our attitudes and behaviors to mirror the heart of Christ. What I offer is a reflection of someone working in the field. I have had successes and failures. I have worked in the vineyard, and from this toil I want to share with you what I have learned and experienced. I hope this book will strengthen you in your ministry of caregiving to the Body of Christ.

I deeply appreciate the help of those who minister to me and with me. My wife, Dorothy, has encouraged and loved me. I thank God for our chaplains and board of directors of Pastoral Care Associates and all those who have befriended me thorough the year.

I pray that Jesus will bless you in the reading of this book and confirm within you that which is true and helpful.

The Rev. Michael Lessard
Phoenix, Arizona—2010

SOMETIMES

Sometimes I wish the path was straight,
and I could walk or run
at a faster gait.

I wish sometimes that simple footsteps could
accomplish more,
that my soul and body did not get sore.

I sometimes wish that I could breathe,
at a pace, a dash of speed,
without a wheeze.

But then I might have missed the view
that special path
that led to You.

Where do You live, Lord?
Foxes have holes, and birds of the air have nests;
But the Son of Man has nowhere
To lay his head. (Matt. 8:20 nrsv)

CHAPTER 1

PROLEGOMENON
(A THEOLOGY OF CARING)

I RECENTLY ATTENDED a clergy conference; you know one of those meetings that cause you to wonder how the church has survived this long. The discussion was about priorities—how much money and attention was to be spent for this or that project and how to invest our human capitol to further God's plans. I have been to many, many meetings like this over the years, but this meeting was very unsettling. Perhaps it's because I am older, or maybe I am going through midlife transition, but it has caused me to think and sit down and write this book. Writing is not easy for me, so to get me motivated takes some sort of epiphany. Hopefully, the Holy Spirit has had something to do with it.

I have had a lot of ideas running around in my head and I have given many teachings over the years. Now seems to be the time to share them. I intend to show in a systematic way that caring with the heart of Jesus is the central element permeating everything the Church teaches and does. I thank God that I can make this small offering. It has taken countless hours of clergy conferences, vestry meetings, and assorted painful planning sessions for this moment of liberation and clarity.

A CHRISTOLOGY OF CARING

The primary ministry of Jesus was pastoral care, healing, reconciliation, and teaching. The Gospels are inhabited with the evidence of Jesus' care and love. We experience Him doing the ministr y of caring, and we see Him training and sending others out to continue this ministry. For example, when he sent out the seventy-two in Luke 10:1-12, He gave them instructions. He also directed his apostles in the same way. He ordered them not to bring anything with them except the peace they offered at the door.[1]

Jesus did not evangelize as we think of evangelizing today. He preached the Kingdom of God and invited some to follow. What really separated Him from the Old Testament prophetic tradition was His tremendous ministry of caring for the sick and healing them. Jesus has experienced our pain. He did not avoid the human condition but entered into the drama of human suffering. He understood it well because He sought it out. He went into the desert and was tempted for forty days and nights.[2] He openly discussed His death on the cross.[3] He was and is a man acquainted with grief, as Isaiah says. It is because of the truth of the humanity and divinity of Jesus that we have a Christology of a Savior who cares for us.[4]

A Christology of caring is incarnational. Jesus began His human journey as we all begin, and as creation itself emerged from the womb of God's creative energy. Physicists, beginning with Lamaitre, Friedman, Hubble, and others have been able to identify that the universe is expanding and moving away from us. They hypothesize that the universe began with a tiny particle of matter that kicked off the process of creation. This seed of matter, this singularity, became an ever expanding space as gas and planets formed, suns ignited, and the physical laws of nature began to operate.

Every person begins with a tiny moment of creation. God entered our humanity, in the same way, through this microscopic door of materiality. He is born just as every person is born. Cells begin to multiply and they divide. The heart begins to pump blood and oxygen and cells grow into an embryo. He became Emmanuel, God with us. God is not distant or detached. He engages us from our most fragile beginnings. He makes our beginnings His own. He is not content to let creation go its own course. He chooses to get inside it and make it sacred. Jesus describes this love of God, this faith in creation, as a mustard seed. He invites us into the world of wonder and trust. He introduces us to the pregnant possibility that makes all things possible.

The Kingdom of God is found in the Incarnation of Christ. This is the seed that grows the revelation of God's personal care for us and for all things. It recognizes human suffering and our limited mortality—the reality of life and death. (Tillich calls it the polarity in which we all live.)[5] Jesus enters into our human Jerusalem. He experiences the polarities of being adored by the crowd outside the walls of the city and all the while the Pharisees are plotting His death inside the walls of Jerusalem. Jesus embraces our humanity; life and death willingly and chooses it with all its consequences. Saint Paul tells us in Romans 8:34 that the only reason Jesus would make such a leap is because He loves and cares for us. His choosing the incarnation cements us to Him in love and care. The result of this incarnational leap is that He is not difficult to live with and He is not caught up in himself. Pain and suffering don't diminish Him. He is a joy to be with because He is so real.

Jesus never hides behind anyone or anything. He does not posture, pretend, or run from conflict. He does not give up. He does not use people or bow to public opinion. If Jesus is on your side, you know where He is going to be—right next to you. The Scriptures say that He intercedes for us before God the Father.[6] That is the kind of defender I need and want. He has paid the price for you and me, and He has the scars to prove it. He chooses and redeems all of humanity's sin, pain, suffering, and death.

I have been a hospital chaplain for twenty years. The measure of my ministry is not what I have done or accomplished, but what I have witnessed. Christian caregiving is incarnational. It is where I meet the Lord. Jesus is in the patient on the ventilator who cannot speak, but who raises a hand to me as I walk into the room. He is in the person who is alone or frightened by an upcoming surgery. He is in every patient, in every prayer, and in every doctor, nurse, and family member. Perhaps it is because I see Him so often in each person, I can appreciate how every human encounter is an opportunity for grace to break through and warm our heart with meaning and truth.

No interaction between people is an accident because each person contains a divine invitation to care for one another. Small talk that seems relatively mundane can lead to a moment of vulnerability thin turn leads to a moment of God's blessing and love.

One of those ice-breaking questions that people often ask is, "What do you do for a living?" It can be asked on the golf course or at a party or social function. When I tell them that I am a hospital chaplain, the next question is, "Isn't that depressing? How do you keep from getting depressed?" The questions seems to suggest that hospital chaplaincy should be difficult and a heartache. I usually say that most of the patients at the hospital recover. If they didn't, no one would ever go there. The fact is, I am impressed, not depressed. Pastoral care is incarnational.

I have the privilege of being with people at moments of great sorrow and pain, joy and exaltation. I am aware that I stand on holy ground where God and human beings meet in the crucible of human suffering, or in the exaltation of new life or recovery. It is the sanctuary of the Temple. It is the Mount of Olives. It is the open door to paradise. My wife has said that, "Eternity is just outside our skin." I have had the experience of being with and praying for those whose journey to Christ happens in a twinkling of an eye and is just outside the veneer of mortality. The Incarnation ties our journey to the mantle of Christ's journey of redemption. God is not disengaged from our personal experience. He is found in it.

Christians hope in an eternal life with God. We need a pioneer who has gone ahead to cut the path and to blaze a trail for us to follow. Jesus is that Shepherd who cares to lead the way to our eternal homeland. The biblical image of the Christ, the Good Shepherd,[8] shows how committed Jesus is to my pastoral care and to yours. We hear in Psalm 23 that God intends to be entrusted with our care. He will watch over us. He will protect us. He will guide and direct us to good pasture. He will lead us with his rod, an extension of His arm, to keep us together and moving in the right direction.[9]

A Theology of Caring is not permissive. The rod of the Shepherd is to inspect the sheep and keep them in line and in sight safely within the flock. The Good Shepherd has boundaries. He cares for the sheep and sets limits for their own good. "Your rod and your staff—they comfort me."[10]

I can trust God's judgment because His holy will is to lead and guide me to the heart of His love. The cultural pressures of today are so great upon the Church that we are tempted to lose sight of the Good Shepherd and like sheep nibble ourselves away until we are lost.

Our culture offers quick fixes and business style solutions to most problems. The church is being stretched to accommodate modern cultural methods which promote a type of gospel that validates cultural beliefs. We focus our attention on mission goals, media, evangelization, stewardship, buildings, the latest liturgical fad or musical style—whatever the latest Church growth gimmick is. We so compartmentalize church programs that we may be losing the bond of caring that keeps us together. Have we strayed so far away from the Gospel that we can't differentiate the church from the culture? Many have adopted cultural ideas such as targeting groups by age or financial and social status. Have we marginalized our youth by separating them into groups and cliques? Have we adopted a Gospel that accepts things the way they are because we must accept the culture we live in and do business the way it does?

I remember that a newly-elected Bishop said one day at a clergy meeting that he was not a good pastoral care person. We would have to rely on others to meet our needs." You know, that diocese never had a clergy retreat until he retired ten years later. How could that be? How is it possible that someone who promises to shepherd the sheep and lead them to Christ is not a pastoral care person and is not equipped to shepherd the shepherds? He might have other redeeming qualities: he might be a good storyteller, CEO, organizer, and be personally charming. He made a point of trying to be "inclusive" in the moral teaching of the Church, but what about the heart of the Gospel? Perhaps the church has placed too much value on leadership abilities that do not require caring.

It is no surprise Pope John Paul wrote that the culture of death has taken root and grown in our society.[11] When the shepherds give the care of the sheep to a hired man, the sheep run wild, get lost, and suffer death in the jaws of wolves; instead Pastoral care ministry is vital for the life of the Body of Christ because it is the heart of the Gospel.

In my years as a chaplain, I have seen many cardiac resuscitations and code arrests. I believe that the heart is the most important organ in the body. Modern medicine does all kinds of things to keep the heart going. We shock it, we medicate it, and we operate on it because the heart is vital for life to continue. We can only replicate what the heart does for a short time. Without a working heart, the blood fails to circulate to the rest of the organs and they die. When the heart stops, brain death is just minutes away. The patient with no heartbeat and blood pressure is about to experience eternity. The importance of Christian caregiving needs to be recognized as the basis for the heartbeat and life of the Church. The local church will require more pastoral care resources to meet greater and greater demands as the Baby Boom generation continues to move into retirement.

The Church, in recent times, has understood pastoral care as a specialized ministry for a few trained professionals. As a result, it is not sufficiently equipped to meet the growing needs of an aging population. Many churches are now on life support trying to exist with a diminished capacity to give care. It is critical to restore the heart of the Church for us to be revived, renewed, and strengthened. We need to train all the people of God to become ministers of care. An incarnational theology of care means that as Christ has given us His heart of love, and we must respond by caring for one another.[12]

CREATION AND GRACE

In the Book of Genesis, God gave Adam the job of tending the Garden of Eden.[13] Adam was created to be a caretaker. God had created the universe and the world and cared for it. God wanted the man to know the wonder of the world by caring for it as He does. Grace is the benefit of God's love and care. The promise to Adam, even after his sin, was that God still cared.[14] He made clothes for Adam and Eve,[15] and Paul says (1Cor. 15: 20-28) He has restored creation by giving us a new perfect Adam.[16] God cares so much for us that He is willing to put on our skin. He will not only clothe us, but He will put on our clothes. He will put on our humanity. God who lives in eternity will become flesh and blood and He will restore His care to all people for all time.

Sin kills caring. "Am I my brother's keeper?" asked Cain.[17] Selfishness and pride replace caring with self-protection. Lying, cheating, theft, and violence reduce caring to irrelevancy and destroy trust, friendship, and intimacy. More importantly, sin treats God's care as a delusion or a myth. It creates a cynical world whose covenant is with death. It says, "Let's live life to get the most pleasure since tomorrow we will die." Exploitation, drug addiction, and our compulsive habits anesthetize us against facing ourselves and our pain. Some churches try to make faith relevant by soft-peddling sin. This idea undermines our need for redemption and conversion.

In my rounds at the hospital, I have encountered some people who have given up on God. They blame Him for their condition. They are angry and disapproving of any mention of the "G" word. The last thing they want to see is someone who represents Him. Occasionally, I wonder if I have unexpectedly entered HBO's Bill Maher's talk show world of disbelief. These people think that a belief in God is a betrayal of their jealously guarded anger at the difficulties of life. They believe pain and suffering, if there is a God, is a divine trick to force us to accept a drink from the elixir of some semi-benevolent deity. They hold on to a hopeless fantasy of fear. If we deny God's existence, we deny His care for us.

I recently was making rounds in the ICU unit. I visited a patient who appeared to be about sixty years old. He was lying in his bed. I gave him a big hello and introduced myself. His immediate response was, "I am an atheist and I don't believe in what you are selling." I explained to him that I visited all our patients and that I hoped he was starting to feel better. I asked him, "What was the reason for your hospitalization?" He said," I have a bad ticker and I need to have bypass surgery." I said, "When are they going to do the surgery?' "I am going to have surgery in a few hours, and I am not excited about the idea," he said. I looked at him and said as I moved closer, "I hope the surgery goes well for you." I touched his arm. He looked back at me and said, "God willing, it will." No sooner had the words left his mouth, than he wanted them back. He tried to catch them, but it was too late. Out of his subconscious, he blurted out hope. Someone who had cared for him years ago had put those words in there. Now, when he was under stress and in difficulty and hardship and the wolf of death was at the door, here was the truth. God cares and loves and wills life. When we care as God does, and in the way He does (as Jesus is now doing), we put skin on God for ever yone to see. Christian caregiving mirrors the primary sacrament of God's work in creation. That is why Jesus gave care all the time, even on the Sabbath. He put skin on the covenant between Israel and God. He invites us to enter into His graceful caring presence and we delight in His works.

It is no wonder that the first thing that every totalitarian state and every despot, tries to eliminate by killing His servants, is the love of Jesus Christ. The self-serving superior egoist, the powerful tyrant, the immoral hedonist, cannot remove or supplant God's care.

The state cannot serve as a god. Every time man's ego and the state have tried to kill the Christian faith, they have ended up in the ashes of ruin and failure. Every man, woman, and child has a god. But what matters is whether the (G) god they worship the real one or not?

Patients usually tell me within the first few minutes of a visit what kind of (G) god they believe in. They cannot help it. They have to tell their story. Our stories center on themes of redemption, meaning, hope, pain, and they ultimately reflect our personal theology. The caring Christian is one who looks for these personal revelations, listens for them, and lives in the grace of the moment. I have had many conversations with people who recognize that their god is too small, too identified with self, too cloaked in fear, too distant and unavailable to care. It is because I have cared to listen that there have been *aha!* moments. It is because of His grace in my personal story that I can hear the pain and need in someone else's story. The grace for the ministry of caring comes from the cross and resurrection of Christ. The Holy Spirit pours grace on us like oil on our heads.[18] The Holy Spirit hands over to us the ministry of our calling to care for one another through the experience of being adopted as God's sons and daughters.[19]

THE HOLY SPIRIT—CARING CHARISMS

When Jesus fed the five thousand it was because He was full of compassion for those with Him who had been listening to His teaching. We are told that he felt for them because, "They were like sheep without a shepherd."[20] Jesus is affected by people and events around Him. He goes where the Holy Spirit leads Him. It is the Spirit that moves and empowers His ministry. It is the Holy Spirit that fills Him with care for others. He understands the nature of His calling and its duties in the Spirit. The same action of the Holy Spirit comes down upon Him at His baptism and it falls upon the apostles at Pentecost. It is the Holy Spirit who will teach and guide them as they plant the church. The Holy Spirit will be with them in their fellowship, when they gather, and when they care for one another. The Holy Spirit will help them when they need wisdom to say the right things.[21]

When I was a seminarian I had the reputation of being the spokesman for the Holy Spirit. (This was not my idea.) I was a card-carrying Charismatic Catholic and some of my professors used to try to trip me up with theological questions about the Holy Spirit. One day my New Testament professor asked me, "Mr. Lessard, which person of the Trinity raised Christ from the dead?" At first, I was stymied by his question and its tone and I felt defensive. At that moment, I remembered a song from our prayer meetings, "It's the same Spirit that raised Christ from the dead that dwells in you."[21] I said loudly, "The Holy Spirit raised Christ from the dead and that's found in Romans." You know, he never tried to embarrass me in class again.

The Holy Spirit will bring to mind the things you need to remember. The Holy Spirit is God's personal care for the Church. I have wondered why Jesus said that He had to leave for the Spirit to come down to us. Perhaps it was because when Jesus was present in Galilee, we did not need the Spirit. The apostles had the Word of God speaking love and care directly to them. Now we have the same Spirit that raised Christ from the dead who dwells in us through baptism. It is in the Spirit that we remember—the important words of institution that makes Christ present in the Eucharist. We ask the Spirit to come upon us and upon the gifts of bread and wine, making them the body and blood of Christ.[22] It is in the gifts of the Holy Spirit that we experience God's personal care for us. All the gifts of the Spirit reveal the same caring that Christ has shown and is now showing. It is in the Spirit that we worship, prophesy, teach, heal the sick, and minister the compassion of Christ Jesus.

There have been times in my ministry when I have been aware that the Holy Spirit's gift of caring was at work. Sometimes, as I have listened to a patient, the compassion of Jesus was so abundant that I was taken aback by it. I wondered from where the words had come. Certainly not from me. I had been tired or pre-occupied or just busy then suddenly as I listened, the compassion flowed out. Of course, it was not from me. It was the compassion of Jesus, His caring, His Word being poured out in the Holy Spirit. I have had many moments after such a visitation when I have contemplated the great care God has shown me. I thank

Him and praise Him. It is the gift of the Holy Spirit's love that provides pastoral care.

God the Father sent the revelation of His love and care to us in His Son, Jesus. The heart of His Word made flesh is given to us in the Spirit.[23] The gifts of His caring are ministered in the Spirit. If the church is nothing else, let it first be caring. We have no higher calling, no greater vision, no other purpose than to care for one another as Christ cares for us. The church has been baptized into the ministry of caring. It has been purchased by the blood of the Lamb, and it is led by the power of the Spirit to be a witness that God cares for all of humanity.

Things Left After the Flood

Death/Life

       Before/After

              Forgotten/Remembered

Empty/Full

       Moving/Still

             Baptized and Reborn

CHAPTER 2

THE BAPTIZED ARE THE CHURCH

CHRIST POURS THE ministry of caring upon us in the Spirit at our Baptism. We have different natural talents, abilities, and gifts, but one thing that unites us in the Spirit is the gift of caring. The laity is the essential building block of caring in the world. The Church is birthed in our homes, with our spouses, children, and grandchildren. The Church is where we live and who we live with. How we show caring to one another when we are sick, or how we forgive one another when we are hurt, is a witness to our life with Christ. The most important questions we need to consider reside in our homes. How is your "church" doing? Are you getting along with your husband or wife? Is there safety and love for your spouse and children? Are the benefits of your Christian home apparent to those who know you and work with you? In other words, do you care for one another? If the church at home is not a caring place, what is the point of gathering with a bunch of other people on Sunday mornings?

To be real, Sunday worship needs to be congruent with caring for one another in a Christ-like way at home. Other wise, we can easily play church, doing religious things without the substance of caring and loving each other. This is hypocritical. To avoid the error of religious pretense, we need to recognize and use the sacramental power of Jesus available to our families in the Spirit.

THE FAMILY AND THE SACRAMENTS

I realize the role and function of the ordained clergy, so my reflections on the sacraments are intended to strengthen the family. I am describing a paradigm that stresses the significance of the familial bond and its connection to the sacramental life. I do not want to minimize ordained service. On the contrary, I hope to strengthen the foundation that provides a spiritual floor for supporting the vocations that will lead the future church. My reflections can apply to single persons as well as married, since almost everyone has some familial relationships—relatives, close friends, and coworkers can be a part of a single person's church at home.

All the sacraments use signs that families understand as essential for life. We use water (baptism). We gather around the table (communion). We forgive one another (absolution). We bless one another and we provide medicines for healing (anointing of the sick). Marriage is the covenant with life sanctified by Christ's presence in the man and woman that births the future Church. God's care is communicated through signs of love, belonging, and affection. It is important that the first miracle Jesus performed in John's Gospel was at a wedding. He changed water into wine to show that the marital relationship in Christ produces the new wine of caring for and being the Church.

In New Testament times, families were not just a social institution that produced offspring, but a place where the Church was incubated. The wine is the fruit of the vine and the vine is Jesus (see John 15). Marriage is so important that Jesus often refers to Himself as the bridegroom. In the book of Revelation we are told that we are going to marry the Lord. There is an assault against the family today in our culture. We have a fifty-percent divorce rate, confusion about monogamy, and same sex marriage. The effect of this attack is for many to lose hope in marriage as an institution. However, if we lose the family, we lose the church. If the belief in the sacredness of marriage can be devalued, then hopelessness and cynicism will replace love, bonding, and caring in our society. We must equip the family with its sacramental authority and power. It's time, in the way it happened at Cana, that we serve the *new wine*.[24]

Serving the *new wine* begins with communicating the faith in a familial way by doing, showing, and telling. The Church has often put training on the back burner because training is relational and demanding. The Gospels show us that this is exactly how Jesus taught:

He built up the apostles, reflected with them, answered their questions, and ministered to them by caring for them.[25]

We have focused on education as the model for the institutional church. We can teach the faith, but how do we train people in the faith? It is harder to train people because it requires a more hands-on approach to our Christian calling. The medical model, for example, requires not just education, but hands-on supervision. Who wants a doctor who knows about removing a gall bladder, but has not been trained to do the procedure? I would not be willing to entrust my body to someone who has not been trained to operate on it. Yet, we try to raise children, build our families, and try to love our spouses with only a minimal amount of preparation and training.

We are infected with the culture's false sense of immediacy. Many think, Let's get through the pre marriage inventory or the Churches other requirements to have a big Church wedding. Let's get through religious education so we can get First Communion or Confirmation. The number of dropped out or lapsed Christians continues to climb. Why is that? If the educational model was working, we would have a stronger and more vibrant Church. In my opinion, we have to face the fact that the educational model is not sufficient for the task. We need a *new wine* method that centers on the heart of the Gospel—a direction that is caring-orientated and built on a training model of experiential and theological reflection.

Throughout this book I will be sharing with you my own pastoral experience so that hopefully you can learn the characteristics of caring with the heart of Christ. I will show you a way to build a community that is trained in caring with Christ. The methodology of experience and theological reflection that I use will open your heart to experience the love of Jesus and examine the pastoral and sacramental meaning of the church. Many in the church today see pastoral care as one of the many ministries that all churches are supposed to do. I want you to see that caring is who we are. To be a disciple of Jesus Christ, it is essential for the believer to be caring.

Caring means being aware of the needs of the other person. The first step of caring is listening. There are eleven active listening skills that are the basis for developing tools of caring. For many years I have been associated with LEAD PLUS which offers a forty-hour active listening training.[26] The lab is an essential way to start to become a conscious and caring church. I used to think that if I could just train up a few people like the vestry or a few caregivers, we could influence the institutional church model. I have discovered that my thinking was far too small. We need to reshape the whole Church and move toward becoming a caring people. Our theology, liturgy, evangelism, stewardship, and church polity need to be caring centered.

BAPTISM, THE TIE THAT BINDS US TO CARING FOR EACH OTHER

I have many opportunities in my work with patients to examine the experiences in my own life that have changed me and moved me closer to God. The events which have caused me to reflect, have also created a pattern of love in my heart. Sometimes the event can be a surprise, a tearful parting, a joyful reunion, or a transition like a new job or home. It may not be earth-shaking, but it is life-changing. It's a sacramental event. My wife and I adopted our son when he was thirty years old.

He was my wife's nephew and his parents died when he was little. We had raised him and nurtured him to adulthood. Then, one day he called us from Florida and asked why he had never been adopted. My wife said that some people in his father's family had opposed the idea. "Well," he said, "all those people have died." We asked him if he wanted us to adopt him." George said, "Yes, Mom and Dad, I really want to be adopted." So we flew him out to Phoenix and began the process of adoption. A social worker interviewed us. George had to testify before a judge that he was making this decision freely and without coercion. It was a blessing, not just for him to have this bond recognized and affirmed, but also for us, since he had chosen us.

When the court finalized the adoption, we received a new birth certificate with our names on it as his parents. Not only did our son have a new name, but a new past, and a new identity. Something old was gone and something new was now his and ours. We had more than a legal bond. We had a filial bond that identified us as his parents and him as our son. The experience has given us a wealth of blessings.

The Bible compares baptism to an adoption,[27] something old has passed away and something new has taken its place. What has died (passed away) is the covenant with death.[28] What has been birthed is our filial bond with God. The family relationship provides benefits for both parties. We have the Holy Spirit and His gifts. We receive the blessings of familial love with God. We have an identity of priest, prophet, and king through God's grace. We have secured the benefit of being with God forever in heaven.

We receive many more blessings than these, but I would like to focus on one specific benefit that is often overlooked. Baptism drops the scales of sin from our heart, and at baptism, the covenant with death shrivels and dies. We receive a new spiritual heart. We receive God's care in the person of Jesus Christ and He receives us. We are raised up with Him. We care with Him. We join Christ through His grace in the Spirit, and we are given His blessing to care for His creation, to care for each other, and to magnify the Lord in our spirit.[29] The sign and work of this benefit is forgiveness of sin and healing. Every Christian has all of God's favor, blessing, and grace because they are members of His family. We are not impoverished, with regard to grace and caring. We are His sons and daughters. We do not lack in any good work[30] because we are in Christ Jesus, and we abide in Him.[31]

THE MINISTRY OF RECONCILIATION/ FORGIVING AND FORGETTING

It was a scandal to the Jews that Jesus made the claim that He could forgive sin. They knew that only God could forgive sin, yet Jesus not only said so but He also tied His ministry of reconciliation and healing together. If He can make a blind man see, or a deaf man hear, or make a lame man walk with a word, He can absolve sin with a word. Christ's word of forgiveness on the cross was, "Father, forgive them; for they do not know what they are doing."[32] Forgiveness comes from the heart of God. Jesus completes the promise of redemption with a final breath of absolution. We receive the word of forgiveness. We live in it. We celebrate it, and we are called to share it with one another. It is not acceptable to take a ministr y given to ever yone and place it in the hands of a few. We are all ambassadors of reconciliation because we all have received the benefit of Christ's word of forgiveness (see 2 Cor. 5:17-25). Caring as Jesus does means forgiving as Jesus does.

An ambassador is one who speaks Christ's word of forgiveness in the same way that God speaks it to us. When the President of the United States appoints an ambassador to another country, that person speaks with the same voice as the President. His or her task is to represent the policies of the United States. If the embassy is attacked, or the ambassador is assaulted, it is an act of war because it is like attacking the United States of America.

The calling is for all Christians to speak the word of forgiveness that we have received from Christ Jesus our Savior. We cannot advance the Kingdom of God if we are reluctant to forgive as God forgives. On the other extreme, it is not acceptable to tell others to just ask God to forgive their sin, when we are unwilling to amend our behavior or to forgive the other person.

Sin needs to be admitted for what it is. It needs to be raised to consciousness and confessed to the person we have offended. There are three steps to forgiveness:

1. I must know I did something wrong.
2. I need to be sorry for the pain and hurt I have committed against someone.
3. I need to have a purpose of amendment. What am I going to do differently so I don't continue in the same pattern of behavior?

I have three primo chaplain parking spots at the hospital right in front of the Emergency Room. The words" Clergy Parking" are clearly painted on three signs at these three spots. One day a physician came up to me and said, "Chaplain, I am sorry but I parked in one of your spots." I said, "Do you promise not to do it again?" He looked at me with a sheepish grin that admitted guilt while expecting unremitting forgiveness. He shrugged his shoulders and said, "Well, no." And I said, "Well, then, you are not sorry."

We both had a good laugh about this incomplete confession. You see, for repentance to be real, all three aspects must be a part of it. Repentance means a turning around of my behavior. It is not just admitting guilt and remorse, it is being willing to change. Repent means to go back to the high ground or to the top floor of the relationship before the conflict or hurt or sin. It literally means to reclaim the full benefits of the relationship when it was its most productive and intimate.

Prayer is our communication with God. It is our love language. Some in the church have made a penance out of prayer and prayer a penance. No wonder that the use of the Sacrament of Reconciliation has diminished when we have the impression that our prayers are an attempt to appease God's judgment. Prayer is how we enter into His caring presence and it is the way we commune with Him.

Reconciliation is a grace that flows from God's caring so that our relationships can recover when they have been broken as a result of sin. If my wife and I have an argument where we are both hurt by the tone and the words spoken, it may imperil our relationship. How can we make it better? How do we repair the brokenness and disruption? What do we do with that knot in the pit of our stomachs, the anxiety that says things are not right? My wife, Dorothy, and I have realized that separately we need to take an inward look.

Whenever there is a fight, there are two people who could have done something different. I ask myself what I could have done differently. What am I sorry for that hurt her? What will I do to avoid this behavior in the future? I ask myself these questions not for her, but for me, and she does the same. The answer to these questions becomes apparent with a little reflection, and then I am ready to seek forgiveness from her. She does the same. We take turns listening while the other person confesses the sin—that which each of us is sorry for and what is our purpose of amendment (repentance).

There is one more important final step. It's called absolution. The word means to untie the knot. It is blessing the person with God's forgiveness. Absolution disentangles the pain of rejection, hurt, resentment, and the need for control that comes with human protection. God not only forgives my sin when I ask Him, but He puts it in His holy forgetfulness. We need to forgive and forget because God cares for us this way.

The Prayer of Absolution is forgiving in the heart of Jesus. We become His hands and His mouth and His word of forgiveness. It is an experience of great release and love for the person receiving it and for the person giving it. Forgiveness is reflexive. You get it when you give it, and you give it when you get it.[33] Dorothy and I use the same prayer of absolution that the priest uses in the Catholic Church. However, the Prayer of Absolution in the 1979 *Book of Common Prayer* is just as good:

> God the Father of Mercies through the death and resurrection of His son Jesus sent the Holy Spirit among us for the forgiveness of sin. Through the ministry of the Church may He grant you pardon and peace and I absolve you of all your sins in the name of the Father and of the Son and of the Holy Spirit. Amen[34]

The laity are in need of this Prayer of Absolution. We are meant to use it for each other. I can witness to you that when Dorothy and I use the Prayer of Absolution, and after we go through the three steps of forgiveness, we don't remember our last conflict. We are always blessed in our relationship because we experience God's care for us through the other. The prayer contains these key elements:

- It is through God's mercy and because of the sacrifice of Jesus that the Holy Spirit is sent among us for the forgiveness of sin.

- All of us are participants in this ministry. We are the Church, and it is the ministry of the Church to do reconciliation.

- The benefits of absolution are pardon and peace. These are also the fruits of the resurrection of Jesus.[35] "Peace I leave with you; my own peace I give you."[36] We minister what we have received.

There is no greater gift given to the Church than this power to forgive sin. It is the last word Jesus tells us in the Gospel— the power to bind and to loose.[37] We can loosen the knot and let ourselves and others go free in the grace of forgiveness. Jesus died on the cross for our sins, but He rose again on the third day and sent the Holy Spirit so that we may be ministers of reconciliation.

We all are empowered through our baptism to be priests to one another and to exercise the ministry of His reconciliation. We say the words of absolution as we place our hands on the head of the person who is seeking our forgiveness. The appropriate place to give and receive absolution is with our family. This is not to diminish the sacrament of reconciliation with an ordained priest or bishop. They stand in as proxy for the person we can't find or get to. We should not release a person's responsibility to give or receive absolution from the person they have offended. Without its proper context, the familial nature of the sacrament gets lost, and it can quickly become a litany of offences without meaning or real repentance. Without the foundation of caring, reconciliation can easily devolve into pietistic posturing. Perhaps confession has been put on the shelf until we discover its rightful place in the heart of our families and relationships. The fruit of the Sacrament of Reconciliation promotes healing relationships that are congruent with the love of Jesus within the family.

THE MINISTRY OF HEALING/ HEALING OUR HURTS

Over my years in pastoral care, I have prayed with many people for healing. I have seen miracles and witnessed God's power at work. I am reminded that in the Gospel Jesus prays for the sick and the hurting all the time.[38] We are following our great High Priest, Jesus, who has entered the Holy of Holies and is present for us when we pray for each other. I have ministered inner healing to people and I have found that healing follows after or through reconciliation.

The healing of memories is asking Jesus to go into the memories of hurt or pain in our childhood or into some painful event that wounded us (even as far back as the womb). We ask Him to heal our memories of the past. There have been many books written on the subject of inner healing.[39] The most important place to do inner healing is in our homes and families because the home is the primary church. Husbands and wives need to pray inner healing for and with each other. In the book, *Getting the Love You Want*, the author says (to paraphrase) that we pick someone to marry who we trust to heal our childhood wounds, to help us to make sense of our pain, and to be cared for by someone who is safe. Our husband or wife is the person we have selected to be a minister of God's healing to us.[40]

Pre–marital preparation needs to be centered on several important skills. Active listening training is paramount in how to listen and practice these skills in your marriage (listed on page 100)[41] Inner Healing, which is asking Jesus to heal our memories when some pain in the past affects the present; Reconciliation and Absolution, how to give and receive forgiveness from each other when we sin and hurt each other. The kind of training I describe will equip our families with the power of the sacraments and with the skills to care for one another.[42]

Sometimes a person has no close immediate family. In that case, a trained priest or pastoral caregiver can pray for a person in need of inner healing. Here is an example:

> A young lady of about twenty three years old somehow heard about me and traveled from Massachusetts to have inner healing. We met. She had braces on her neck and on all the joints of her arms and legs. She told me that she had not eaten solid food in six years because she had bleeding ulcers in her stomach. She wanted to know if I would help her—if prayer could help her. She was under the care of several doctors that had diagnosed her condition as a rare form of arthritis and psoriasis that affected her skin with terrible rashes.
>
> As we prayed, her story began to emerge. Her mother had left her when she was two years old. She was taken in by her grandparents who were kind to her, but she felt a lack of love and emotional attachment to them. Both of her grandparents had significant arthritic conditions. I asked her about what age she was when she began to develop her symptoms. She said, "I was about eighteen when it started." I asked how old her mother was when she left her with her grandparents. She said her mother was about eighteen or nineteen.

As I prayed for Jesus to heal her memor y of the terrible abandonment of her mother, I received a mental image of a chain wrapped around her that was attached to her grandparents' arthritis. As we prayed together over the hurt and pain, one by one she took off her braces and she experienced the healing grace of Jesus releasing the chain of arthritis and restoring her bones and joints.

I didn't tell her she had to forgive her mother, but she realized that as we prayed. She began to forgive her mother and her stomach pain disappeared. It was a moment of great excitement when she realized that she was healed. She jumped up and danced around praising God. Then, for the first time in six years, she asked for food and ate without any problem. Jesus gave her the grace to begin the process of healing.

We are not finished. We are a work in process. We need to ask for healing each day. God is working His perfecting will in us. We need all the tools He has provided to work out our salvation. It would be foolish to believe that this woman never felt abandoned again. I am sure she is tempted occasionally by similar circumstances, relationships, or stress, to define herself by her sickness or her painful abandonment.

Jesus asks Peter three times, "Simon son of John, do you love me?"[43] Was Jesus trying to hurt Peter by reminding him of His denial and abandonment? I don't think so. I think that He wanted Peter to remember and recognize the wound in his heart.

From our wound comes compassion. From a personal disappointment comes the ability to feed the sheep because caring is born not by our strength, but in and through our weakness. If Peter is going to lead the Church, he must do so in a transparent way. He must remember not to condemn himself or become bitter, but to live in the gratitude of forgiveness. Paul says he boasts about his weakness. Three times he talks about the fact that he was out to do violence to the Church. Jesus met him on the road to Damascus and changed his life and direction.[44]

I have interviewed all our chaplains and interns, and we all have a wound that Jesus has touched. It is in the private garden of our heart that the tree of compassion is watered and grows. It is in this Gethsemane that we choose to follow Jesus. No one wants to go there, to stay awake there, to suffer there. It is a divine invitation. You and I are invited through grace to care with the heart of Jesus; to reclaim the holiness lost in the first garden and now restored by the second Adam.

THE POWER OF BLESSING

Blessing is a power we are given in baptism. We can bless our children. God knows they need it. We can bless our husband or wife; God knows he or she needs it. We can bless people, objects, and animals. We can bless our food. We can bless our brothers and sisters and our parents. In the Old Testament a son's inheritance was passed on with a blessing from the patriarch (see Gen. 27:12ff). We can pray for healing and we can pray a blessing because through our baptism we have been given the inheritance of sons and daughters of God. If God has given us the ability to absolve sin, certainly we can pray for healing and we can pray blessings upon our wives, husbands, children, and parents.

Please remember, a silent blessing will not do. Put your hands on the head or shoulders of the person for whom you are praying and bless them with a prayer that comes from a caring and generous heart. The absence of blessing is a serious spiritual deprivation. Without it, we find ourselves falling into routines of judgment and even cursing our children. We say things like: "Grow up," "Be a man," "You are bad," "You will never succeed," "You disappoint me." We may even use the Bible to press home our point.

It is vital for family members to be blessing one another. Otherwise we tend to wound our future by condemning the past. If we instill fear in our children, we should not be surprised when we get anger and resentment in return. Life commandments that block our future, harm our identity, are often transformed into sickness or compulsive sins. Blessings bring peace, love, and joy. The first thing Jesus did after He was raised from the dead was to bless the apostles and to offer them peace.[45]

AT THE GARDEN

In the darkness, in the solitary moment, in the tortured emptiness,

He faced the world; He faced the pain of sin; He faced me.

He was the cup of Passover left for Elijah,

The empty Chair

Alone, while we sleep

He accepts the Cross

CHAPTER 3

THE SACRAMENT OF THE HOLY EUCHARIST/
THE FAMILY MEAL

THE GOSPEL STELL us about the feeding of the five thousand. Before Jesus performs this miracle, there is some awareness either by Jesus or the apostles that something needs to be done to feed the people. The little fish and bread that the apostles can produce will not cut it. The people need to be sent away to take care of themselves in town. However, the Good Shepherd is not about to allow the sheep to forage for themselves. They have communed with Him for several days. He has fed their souls, and now He will feed their bodies.

The sign Jesus produces affirms what He has taught. It mirrors His caring love for the sheep. Communion with Jesus is not so much a Passover, but a passage into the heart of God. When Jesus celebrates the feast with His apostles (His friends) before His death, the meal was not a memorial like a funeral announcement. They are not sitting around looking at a scrapbook of old memories. Communion is a pathway for us to enter into what it means to be bonded to Jesus. It is the living bread and the wine of shared lives. We are the guests and He is the host. We share a common family and a common destiny. We share in the cup of His blessing and the cup of His suffering (see 1 Cor. 10:16). We share in His caring for the whole human race.

The family meal is not meant to be a solitary experience. For my family, supper has always been a time for catching up on the news of the day, a time to share concerns, plans, and dreams. Our family meal is that special time when we get together to reclaim our shared history and memories.

In Chapter 17 of the Gospel of John, we find the meaning behind the Eucharist. The Synoptic Gospels have the words and setting of the institution of the Lord's Last Supper (see Matt. 26:19ff; Mark 14:16ff; Luke. 22:15ff). The Gospel of John sets the table of caring and fellowship (see John 15:1-17) It is the sign of a familial bond. Jesus washes the apostle's feet and He shows the extent of God's care for each of them and for us. He invites us to do what He does and to care as He does.

John's Gospel walks us through the experience and meaning of abiding in Christ. It teaches that when we receive the Eucharist, we are taking in God's life and accepting our vocation to care for one another (see John 17ff). We are offered; we are consecrated; we are broken and distributed as sacraments of caring to a hurting world. The spiritual by-product of our familial bond in Christ is unity. Unity is not a manmade goal or a self-conscious, tacit duty to perform. Rather, it is the joyful acceptance of God's call—a divine intention to care for you and me. Our response should be to care for one another. Unity rests on God's shoulders. It is His work as a first fruit of the "new wine" of Cana. Christ's death and resurrection bring us into a new Exodus. As the author of Peter says that they have gone from being no people to being God's people (see 1 Peter 2:10). We are invited to change our hearts from the water of self-interest to the wine of caring as God's family.[46] We leave behind the slavery of sin and the desert of iniquity and follow the Good Shepherd into the Promised Land of God's sons and daughters.

THE LITURGY OF CARING/PRAISING GOD AND CARING FOR EACH OTHER

I have felt over the years that the church service of Holy Communion needs a shift of focus. The ritual, the size of congregation, and the demands of schedules often get in the way of expressing the dynamic intimacy of the Holy Eucharist. At mealtime, I don't want to be entertained, I want to listen and be present to my family. Mealtime is a time for caring, of celebration, and affection. Our society has a difficult time recognizing the importance of family mealtime. The fast-paced world of today is full of activities that impede families and keep them from eating meals together. Parents work two jobs, kids are involved in school schedules and other activities. The media of television, texting, and cell phones all make it more difficult to share mealtime together.

The other day my wife and I went to our favorite restaurant. In the booth next to us two people were eating. Not once did they actually talk together. Instead, they conversed on their cell phones talking to other people the whole time. I thought how sad it was that we actually prefer texting or a conversation on a cell phone to a face-to-face personal relationship. Just being together in the same room or around the same table does not guarantee that there is communion. There are four important elements that make relationships communal.

1. The first ingredient is that we gather to remember. My children love to recall our past experiences together and we often retell the same stories again and again to remind us of our common history. Most of the Old Testament rests on the retelling around the campfire of the history of God's involvement in the life of the community. The acts of valor and humor, the grief and defeat, the victories in battle, and the poetry and wisdom of great men and women all remind us that God cares for us.

2. The second key ingredient is offering. We have something to bring to the table. Our children are now grown. When they come to dinner, they bring something to share. It is more than carrots or chicken or cake. They bring gifts that represent themselves. We share together their offerings which represent work, love, and care. It would be highly insulting not to serve a dish that one of my children made, or in some way intimate that we don't need their offering. A lot of Jesus' ministry happened at mealtime. Nothing seems to have upset Him more than a host who would belittle a guest, and not accept the gift a guest brought, even if it was only tears of repentance.

3. The third important ingredient is thankfulness. It is a recognition that it is good to be together. My spirit is benefited from gathering together as God's family. I anticipate mealtime because I am graced by being in relationship with those for whom I care and those who care for me. It is out of this sense of gratefulness for each other that our response to God's invitation to worship is stirred up. It is impossible to be thankful if we do

not care. Conversely, we cannot help but be thankful if we care for one another.

4. The last ingredient that confects the significance of the family meal is asking the Holy Spirit to bless the gifts of food and fellowship. Blessing provokes us to ponder the meaning of our life together in God's family. The Passover meal is full of blessings, offerings, thanksgiving, and remembrance. The Passover recounts the flight from Egypt, God's salvation, and His care for His people Israel. Our blessing of the meal is not just a few short words of appreciation to God. It is the acknowledgement of God's care in providing for us, for bringing us together, for blessing us with life, and for the dependency we have on Him for our future.

These are the patterns that Jesus knew and He invites us to share intimately from our homes to the Eucharistic table on Sunday. The church needs to model the importance of caring that brings us together as God's family.

I went to a noon mass a few years ago, and while the priest was at the altar saying the Eucharistic Prayer, a man fell over in his pew and passed out. Someone quickly called 9-1-1 and the paramedics arrived right away. They began to treat the man and they put him on a gurney and took him to the hospital. Not once, did the priest saying mass stop, attempt to help, or even lead a prayer for the man. He just kept saying the ritual as if nothing had happened; but something had happened and we all needed to stop what we were doing and care about it. The experience has stayed with me. The priest was a good friend of mine and is a good priest. Yet, I am left with one question: How can this be? Here was a glaring need and not even a prayer was said. Caring was not modeled by the leadership during this mass. We need to recognize that everyone in Church is hurting, including the pastor or priest.

We are all under more stress from the expectations of the culture and work than we have ever been before. We are carrying burdens of finance, children, job, sickness, and the general pain of life. We may be ignoring the suffering out there—like the man who passed out. We may not want to see the harsh realities right in front of us. We may begin to think that the job of the Church is to provide cover from life's difficulties. I have seen this spirit of protection creep into the community. It is demonstrated when church members care more about the trappings of religion than about the substance of caring. It happens when small things in the liturgy become hugely important, and when church politics supplant being a family that cares for one another.

Here are a few suggestions for a new paradigm of a caring-centered community:

- Music would be sung by everyone in a service, and singing would be with simple accompaniment. It would focus on songs that are easily memorized. They would be repeated often enough so they could be learned and sung throughout the day.

- Active listening training would be essential. Discipleship means an investment of time beginning with taking a forty-hour class in active listening training.

- Belonging would mean participation in ongoing training and formation.

- Christian Education would center on caring skills and family support would be focused on parenting, reconciliation, inner healing, and ministry development in our families, along with regular catechism training and theological reflection.

- The Eucharistic liturgy would revolve around themes of caring in the homilies, the ritual, and the tone of worship.

- Theological reflection groups would be held regularly to support the work of the community by practicing the skills and supporting its spiritual development.

- The Liturgy would be intergenerational and everyone would participate.

These are just a few ideas to get you thinking. Worship is an expression of caring for the Body of Christ and celebrating our relationship to Jesus and to one another. Over the years of my ministry, I have developed a personal style of worship. I tend to rely on my own personal experiences and stories to share the gospel. I put a lot of value on the pastor or minister being transparent with their difficulties, problems, joys, and disappointments. The pastors vulnerability models caring in Christ and admits our human reality. Good shepherds must learn to sit still when they need to receive ministry from others.

Jesus has this wonderful availability and touch-ability. He does not shy away from the woman who washes his feet with her tears and dries them with her hair. He is not embarrassed by the woman who anoints Him with oil, but allows her to care for Him.[47] Pastors and their families need to receive affirmation and caring from their congregation. It is a gift that benefits all the people of God.

Celebrating the transitions in life—graduation, home comings, birthdays, and anniversaries—are times of gratefulness for God's blessings. The remembrance of important family experiences builds a bond and provides a personal history of belonging that opens us to welcome others into our family.

My wife and I played tennis on Saturday mornings at a local Community College. One morning we needed some new tennis balls. While we were at the shopping mall, we decided we were hungry, so we went into a grocery store bakery to get some donuts and coffee.

When we had entered, we had walked past some men sitting on a bench in front of the market. Everyone knows that if you are going to do some physical activity you need a couple of donuts and coffee to balance out all the calories you will use up playing the match. Besides, we enjoy eating donuts with our tennis. While on our way out of the store, we saw a man holding a large bunch of rolls. You know, the kind all connected together that can easily be pulled apart. I would never buy that kind because I would likely want to eat them all and then I would have to play tennis all day just to have the calories break even.

Well, the guy with the rolls makes eye contact with one of the guys sitting on a bench in front of the store. He asks him, "Are you hungry?" The guy answers, "Yes, I am." So the guy with the rolls tears off about half of what he has and gives it to him. The man who shared his rolls goes to his cab and begins to eat what he had left over. The guy on the bench looks to his left. At the end of the bench is another guy. He walks over and asks him, "Are you hungry?' The man responds and says, "Yes I am." So he breaks off half of the rolls that he has just received and gives them to him.

By this time, Dorothy and I had gotten into our truck and were watching in amazement. The men both went back to their respective ends of the bench and enjoyed eating a breakfast. I thought it looked a lot like communion. You see, we had just been given a teaching from the Holy Spirit. I am a priest and I walked right past them and didn't even notice their need.

The Bible has a parable that Jesus taught: the Good Samaritan (see Luke 10:29-38). I could almost hear Jesus saying, "Now you go and do likewise." I thank God that He taught me this lesson.

Communion is not just something we do on Sundays or some special occasion. It is a benefit of being God's family and we share in it with others. Caring for one another in Christ will lead us into communion and the Holy Spirit will bring us into unity and service. The Scriptures show us that what Christ taught about the meaning of communion begins with His care for the sheep. He extends to us the same invitation to grasp opportunities to care for one another. We are called to give communion by recognizing a need someone has—by sharing from what we have as a response to God's care for us.

Like the man in the story, communion begins with noticing a need to feed someone. The need may be in giving a breakfast roll or a piece of bread. It may be in listening to someone or caring for a sick friend or loved one. It may be a word of appreciation or some act of kindness that welcomes a stranger. The bread of communion is right in front of us every day and in every person we meet.

The primary place where we begin to shape the communion of caring is in the family. It is examined and developed, practiced and reflected upon within those intimate relationships. Training in active listening is a key component to the development of communion in the family. With it comes reconciliation— an essential gift to practice together. Family prayer, church attendance, and other spiritual exercises should focus on caring for one another in Christ. The result of a more conscious connection between communion at home in the family and communion on Sunday morning will bring the sacrament of the

Eucharist into clearer focus. It will take training and education for us to grasp and live out the intentionality of being the Body of Christ. It will require a recommitment to our calling in Jesus to care for one another. It is not acceptable to leave the communion table on Sunday and produce a sour liturgy of hurt around our own communion table at home. It is not acceptable to treat one another with a lack of respect and care at home, and religiously teach respect for the outward show of pretentious piety (see James 1:26ff).

Many people today are at pain at home. Divorce, drugs, and alcohol, and other compulsive habits disturb the sense of belonging and love. The family (church) will need to use all of its sacramental power to deal with the widespread dysfunction we see in our modern culture. Families are tempted to find meaning in the latest gismo, car, or material object to supply a quick answer for the lack of emotional safety and bonding. Quick fixes rarely live up to the hype. They do bring a shortterm feeling of joy or elation, but it doesn't last. Real caring is found in communion with Christ. Communion in Christ leads right into the heart of the Gospel. The experience of God's care leads us by the Spirit and we are graced into communion with one another.

THE SENTINEL

The sentinel awaits
the dawn!

It breaks upon the day
like an ocean wave.

It tells us something
new has arrived.

I wonder about it…
I wonder about today.

It's never the same,
I'm never the same.

Today begins with
Glory.

Like a sentinel I watch,
I wonder, I wait,
I pray.

CHAPTER 4

CONFIRMATION IN CHRIST

FORMATION, TRAINING, AND EDUCATION OF CHILDREN AND ADULTS

PARENTS ARE THE first and most important shepherds who model faith and caring to their children. They make promises when baptizing their children that they will raise them to know and serve Christ.[48] Yet we somehow get the idea that we are supposed to hand our children off to others to educate in the faith. We send them to Sunday school classes just as we would to regular school and inform them about God, the Bible, and religion in general.

We separate them from the regular church service and call them back when everything is over. It's no wonder that when they get to be teenagers, they are already disengaged from church. We have been unconsciously screening them out for years. I visit many dropped-out Christians at the hospital, and I often hear an adolescent, immature complaint that, "My parents forced me to go to church." When I ask them what church was like for them, I'm often told it is viewed as a place for ritual, conflict, and a necessary obligation to appease their parent's control. The Church is perceived by many in same way they understand the world. It has the same impact in their life as any other institution. It has a unique set of expectations and goals, but its basic operations and functions are no different from any other corporation or social agency.

I often hear this cry for help, and this anger and resentment as an indictment. Behind it is a child who wants to be cared for and loved. The child would like to believe, but has given up hope that the church cares. The Church has many wonderful people who work very hard to communicate the Gospel. It has many fine groups and organizations that care for people. However, we have to admit that far more people are dropped out than are dropped in. There are more inactive than active.

I think that the largest single denomination is the dropped-out Christian. The problem becomes apparent on Ash Wednesday, Easter, or Christmas when the church is full, but the following week I am left with the question, where is everyone? I wonder if maybe we need to give out ashes every Sunday. It feels as if there is some kind of pseudo religion that we have adapted as the Gospel. It is exemplified by a common Sunday routine when some parents drop off their kids for Sunday school and pick them up after church but the parents themselves never attend. The mantra of this pseudo religion, "Religion is good for you and unnecessary for me," translates to a young person as hypocrisy. The effects of these mixed messages are a lack of bonding because they create a sense of mistrust and unsettled conflict that erodes safety and belonging.

The numbers of dropped-out young adults is staggering. In the book, *Already Gone*, by Ken Ham and Britt Beemer, the research of George Barna is cited. They state that twenty percent of churched teens remain spiritually active. Sixty-one percent churched as teens, disengage during their twenties. Only nineteen percent of young adults were never churched as teens and still remain unconnected.

I have to admit that the church has tried, with good intentions, to educate children in spite of the effects of this pseudo religion. Research from Barna indicates that the efforts have worked only for a small percentage of the population. I fear that what we have done by taking over the responsibility for training and educating children instead of letting the parents be the trainers is that we have sown the seeds of their future disillusionment and disassociation.

The work of discipleship training begins in the family. Parents must be trained to teach the faith to their children. Having children means not just raising them to grow up physically, but to grow up in Christ. Confirmation of a calling to follow Jesus and care for the children is the responsibility of the parents. The larger Church can provide materials and training, but the Gospel is incubated at home. The baptismal calling on the parents' life is the same calling in the children's life. We confirm our commitment to Christ with every choice we make.

Confirmation has been viewed by many as a kind of completion of our Christian education, a baseline of knowledge that will get one through life. The truth is that we confirm our calling everyday. Confirmation needs to be a more conscious part of our daily walk with Jesus. A caring-centered theology will recognize that when the bishop lays hands on you for ministry, you better be prepared and trained to care for others.

We all know the horror stories of a young person who was confirmed and then never seen at church again. I sometimes wonder if there is a marketing firm out there making sure that confirmation means that it's okay now to drop out of church.

Confirmation in Christ is a vocational step of caring in Christ. It is not just an educational step like graduating from eighth grade. It is now a way of life confirmed by God and witnessed by the bishop and the people of God. It is a discipleship step into a life of caring with the heart of Christ. We must resist any attempts to make confirmation a pseudo religious educational exercise. One way to counter the temptation of this religious culture is to involve the elderly disciples—the grandparents—in mentoring and training the young.

I like Robert Bly's book *Iron John*[49] because it tells us about the importance of the grandfather in validating a young man's potential (and I include the grandmother to the young woman). Mentoring a young person in the faith includes grandparents and the extended family including godparents. I have seen children trained in this way who at six years of age grasp the meaning of their calling in Christ, can articulate it, and witness to it by caring for others.

Many of our elderly are left out of ministry. They may feel useless or limited by hearing loss or poor eyesight or physical illness. It gets to be difficult to go to church. They may have moved into an adult community to be with people their age only to find themselves lonely and empty. I have interviewed thousands of elderly persons who no longer go to church. Their reasons usually revolve around their physical limitations. Sometimes the reasons include the personal loss of a religious community since they moved from their home back east. Phoenix is a melting pot and a limbo for the elderly. I have interviewed thousands of them. Few actually reconnect to a church, and most view their time of participation in church as over. The result is that many older persons actually participate in church less and less the older they get.

The senior population is a growing group that has dropped out of the church. Many suffer from alcoholism, loneliness, suicide, displacement, and depression, along with all the physical limitations that come with old age. I have heard this complaint many times, "I don't think that this is what God had in mind for our golden years." The elderly not only need to receive ministry, but they also need to give care to the little ones. They need to feel bonded to the future by investing and participating in it. They need to affirm the gifts and talents of the children and pass on the lessons of the Gospel that they learned in their life. The richness of their experience will so bless our children that they would never leave the Source of such a gift. Can this happen in the Church? Only if we care as Jesus cares for us.

CONFIRMATION AND ORDAINED MINISTRY/LEADERSHIP AND SERVICE

When I was ordained, the first words my father said to me were, "Congratulations, son you are now part of the problem." I have not forgotten this prophetic forecast. It reminds me about how quickly I can forget the purpose of ordination—how easily I can become the stumbling block instead of the shepherd. God's calling and His gift of a vocation to the priesthood is not a separation from the laity. Priests are not a different class of heavenly citizens. Many in the world view the ordained minister this way, as a magical touchstone—someone to accede to on those rare occasions when spiritual guidance is required.

Patients in the hospital may ask, "Am I going to die?" They may apologize for their language or make jokes about going up in the elevator with a priest. They may make awkward statements that conclude with a laugh that's more about tension than humor. I have often wondered why the priesthood is so foreign to so many people? One way to avoid an uncomfortable response is to remove the sign of profession from public life. So clergy stop wearing a collar. We stop praying in schools. We stop showing religious symbols in public and remove them from public buildings. And the less the sign is seen, the darker the world becomes. An ordained minister today needs to be available as a visible sign that God is around. Society needs a witness to the caring nature of Christ. Deacons, whether transitional or permanent, need to wear the collar. People need to know who the shepherds are and how they can find them.

If the world is uncomfortable with the sign of caring, let it be!

I was called by the pre-op staff to see a patient. I responded to the page and went immediately. She was in a bed and was surrounded by her family. I walked up to her and suddenly she began to cry loudly. Her family immediately acted as if I had done something terrible to her. They began to tell me that I should stay away and that my presence was not necessary.

Before I could say a word, she said," No, I am glad he is here. I called for him to come, and I needed a good cry." Just my presence as a pastor evoked feelings that she found difficult to express to her family. Now we would pray about the surgery, and all her family would join in.

An ordained person needs to know that signs are important, whether they are understood or not. Signs introduce spiritual things into any situation. Historically, they have been used to designate authority or education or a religious group or order. The primary purpose of ministry is to show the caring heart of Jesus. Perhaps the reason why people get so uncomfortable is because they do not know how to react to the notion that God cares for them. There is that unexpected moment, when for a second, God has put on a little skin. He is not above the human condition, but He is in it with us.

The gift of ordination is familial in nature, since the calling comes, most of the time from the family context. Most of the apostles had wives and families. Jesus did not call them in spite of their families.[50] He called them and invited them to come with Him because they had learned something within their families.

Celibacy can be an important gift for a shepherd. The Roman Catholic Church puts a high priority on this gift. It is also true that the marriage of a calling to ordained ministry and a spouse is also a gift to the Church. It is a witness to the caring love of Jesus who reveals his calling to the entire family. A priest, deacon, or bishop is produced by caring familial relationships. God's revelation is a gift to all families. Jesus affirms the calling of the family and He models the priesthood of all believers to families. The Anglican Church and the Church of Rome are discussing a reunification. In such a case, it is important to allow for our separate traditions to be a blessing for each other. Married clergy have a gift to offer as does the celibate clergy. It is my hope that soon the day will come when we can celebrate the blessed communion that comes from our mutual confirmation of God's Word in unity. The establishment of the permanent deaconate has raised the awareness of the gift of marriage to ordained ministry.

The requirement that the priesthood and Episcopal ministry have been primarily celibate is an unnecessary deprivation to the heart of the Body of Christ's family. I have been married for thirty years. There are many times when my ministry has benefited by my wife's caregiving. It is not just with our children or with the church women. It is not just support and prayer. It is so much more than all those things. Roman Catholic priests have not had the benefit of the experience of marriage, and like someone who missed out on something important, it is easy to dismiss its value. I offer to you three examples of her caring ministry. My hope is that you can appreciate how a wife's ministry and calling is part of her husband's priestly vocation and he is also a part of her priesthood.

THREE SHORT STORIES OF MY WIFE'S CARING MINISTRY

One Sunday my wife and I decided to go to an Italian restaurant after church for a little date. Our waiter came and served us water and we prepared to order. He came back and took our order, but before he could leave my wife said to him, "Are you all right? I saw you holding your stomach before you brought our water." He said, "No, I am not okay. You see, my wife is in the hospital. She had a miscarriage and we lost our little baby. I have felt sick all morning."

Dorothy said, "Michael you need to pray over this man and anoint him with oil." I was glad to do just that and we prayed with him, hugged him, and consoled him. I thought how perceptive of her to notice his sorrow. I had not even made eye contact with him, but my wife recognized his pain and cared enough to ask about it, and we ministered to it together.

On another occasion, we needed to go to the store to pick up a few items for dinner. I was in a hurry and wanted to get home. I rushed on ahead of my wife, who goes at a slower pace sometimes—especially when there is a store full of stuff to look at. I picked up what we needed a few aisles down and came back to see if I could locate her. This is not always easy, especially in a large store. Sometimes, because I can't find her, I have had the feeling that she might have been raptured and left me behind. Today she was right where I left her and she was talking to a young attractive black woman about her beautiful hair, which was neatly braided. She went on about how she loved her glasses and how pretty she was. I thought at first that it was someone she had met before, perhaps in one of those previous raptures. The young woman looked at my wife as if she had known her forever and she began to tear up. She said, "I just got out of prison and these glasses are the ones the state gave me." Again out came the oils and there in the store we prayed together and ministered to her.

Being a priest in a small town is not always easy. I was the rector to a small congregation in rural Arizona. Things had not gone well for me there. My wife was the secretary for the town mayor who was also a lawyer and a member of our church. Being a rector of a small congregation is like being a football coach. If you have a good season you stay, if not, you might as well move on. We were moving on, and with the move came a sense of grief and futility. We faced an uncertain future. So, on this day, I was out doing what any sane priest would be doing when he is facing failure and uncertainty. I was playing golf at the town's nine-hole country club for the last time.

I faintly heard my name being called, and across from the last green my wife waved at me and called my name. I hustled over thinking that something was wrong. When I reached her, she told me that a business partner of her boss had come to town from Denver, Colorado, to see him, but he was in Phoenix. The man was very disappointed. He had traveled a day and a night, gone through snow, rain, and washed-out roads to come here and make his meeting. "Well," Dorothy told him, "there must be some other reason that you are here."

After much conversation and sharing, she asked him, "Have you been baptized?" He said, "No, but he had desperately wanted to be for many years." She gave him some instruction at the office about baptism. She said to me, "Honey you need to get your clubs and meet us at the church and baptize this man God has sent to us all the way from Colorado."

I hurried home, changed, and met them at the church where I baptized him. He was so grateful that first he cried, and then his face lit up like a light bulb. He just beamed! I will never forget that day when out of failure and pain we saw the glory of God. It made leaving that town a precious gift, and a witness to God's faithfulness. The priesthood is enhanced in the genuine calling of a couple to minister caring to the Body of Christ. If I had been celibate, I would have missed these opportunities, but as a married priest, I participated with my wife in my role of shepherd and caregiver.

Ordination to the priesthood models the ministry of caring within the family to the larger family of God's people. We should consider a training and education regime that places more intention on active listening, pastoral care training, and theological reflection on the pastoral situation. Theological study needs to be more grounded on the experience of care. If we are not able to give pastoral care to the flock, what does the rest mean?

I love the world of ideas and insight. If I didn't, I wouldn't be writing this book. Many clergy never leave the pursuit of learning. It can become a way of avoiding caring. However, these two things belong together. Case study learning is a great method of sparking growth and discussion. Couple that with theological reflection and it directs and moves the student to a grounded application of the Gospel. It counterbalances the way intellectual pursuits can disengage us from the concrete here and now.

After my ordination when I started preaching, I thought I was giving great homilies. My wife was in the congregation, and she has told me that she had no idea what I was talking about in those sermons with all the big words. Caring means that we enter the world of the other person by listening and we try to identify with their pain or joy and bring to it the redemptive love of Jesus. Our education can be a defense against doing the hard work of caring for another person.

Bishop, priest, and deacon will need all the tools they can develop and practice to become skilled in the art of caring. The world needs to see the compassion of Jesus in the work of the ministry. We need to reflect on the Scriptures as a road map that directs our actions in caring for one another. Prayer is an essential characteristic of caring. The way our life is a prayer will impact the way we care for one another. Listening to each other begins with listening to God. Jesus took time away from His work of caring to reflect on the Father's care for Him.[51]

WINTER RUN OFF

We harvest the winter water.

Snow has seeded the ground of summer with a new year's supply of possibilities.

In the valley, we trust that water comes from winter to brooks, to rivers, to lakes, to us.

It is a cycle we repeat: we save, we depend on, we hope for, and we need!

Lord, You know about my winter-water harvest. The suffering that is cold and frozen, that waits Your warming touch.

From the harvest comes Your blessing that seeds new possibilities and waters my soul with hope.

Out of the believer's heart shall flow rivers of living water. (John 7:38)z

CHAPTER 5

OUR LIFE OF PRAYER/LOVING *THE GOD WHO CARES FOR US*

THE USE OF incense has never really been an effective symbol for me. I understand its connection to the burnt offerings in the Old Testament,[52] and the meaning of our prayers going up to God as the incense goes up in smoke. Perhaps it is because I have had asthma since I was a little kid and smoke makes me gag. It may be that smoke means fire and fire can mean danger. Lately, I have had to examine my attitudes about incense. I have come to recognize that my life of prayer has this element of interceding for the patient as if it were incense going up to God. I am drawn into their story by listening and to prayer as a response to the patient, family member, or staff member. The pastoral care minister prays all the time and he looks for moments of incarnational connection between God and this patient. The aroma of God's presence is subtle and elusive. Like smoke, it is delicate and communicates the pleasant sense of God's presence. The pastoral caregiver needs to be skilled in sensing God's timing. The fire has to catch hold and start the incense burning.

I have noticed that prayer starts inside a warm heart. Words make the warmth public, and at the same time the Word moves from outside the heart to inside our Spirit. It is not an accident that we are told in the Old Testament, "Speak, for your servant is listening."[53] When we listen to God, the fire of love can become hot enough to produce the flame that kindles the incense. If this attitude of listening to God is so important, we should be trained to offer a good ear to the God of mystery who speaks.

LORD LET ME LISTEN TO YOUR WORD

Jesus tells us, "Let anyone with ears to ear listen."[54] Of course, the people of His day had ears, but did they listen? Do we? Every person has a pattern of speech. It's not just the words they say, but the tone, inflection, pitch, speed, and pauses. These often communicate much more than just the verbal content. I think that God has a rhythm, a tone, and a manner of speaking that reaches out to us. Jesus put his Word and his works together. Both what he said and what he did confirmed the truth of His relationship with His Father. Jesus took the tone of obedience. He sacrificed His will to do the Father's will.

Jesus not only listens to the Father's voice, but to the voice of men and women. He is caught off guard when he hears faith being spoken by a pagan Roman centurion or from a Canaanite woman.[55] Jesus is not afraid to pray in public. He wants to move us into His pattern of prayer, its sounds, its content, and its rhythm. He introduces us to the Our Father.[56] He teaches us the Beatitudes and prays for the resurrection of Lazarus.[57] Jesus cares for us by praying for us. His prayer is the foundation of His sense of belonging to God.[58] The Holy Scriptures reveal the content of God's caring love for us. The Word of God speaks now to you and me. Prayer is a dialogue with God inspired by His Holy Spirit.[59] Christian caregivers mirror the content of God's Word in their prayers. Their prayers flow from the grace of God's pattern in Christ. That is why the Church prays so well—the Eucharistic prayers, the prayer for Anointing the Sick, the prayer of Absolution in Reconciliation, and many others match the content, tone, and rhythm of Christ's pattern of life.

I had a friend who had a great positive influence on me. I admired his knowledge and humility. He was a doctor and a mentor to me. His influence in my early priesthood was profound. I picked up some of his speech patterns, tone, and some of his unique mannerisms. My wife said one day, "Do you know that you are sounding and acting just like Ken?" I had to admit she was right, and even to this day when I am listening to a patient, I find myself bobbing my head up and down as if to say, "Yes, tell me more," just as he did. I desire that Christ's pattern and content will be the primary facility in my life, otherwise my words will be only mine, and they will fall on a deaf world that will not hear because it is too preoccupied to listen.

Prayer that starts in the heart of the Gospel of caring, carries power when it is made public. It is not based on human wisdom, but reflects the heart of God. It heals, it teaches, it inspires to holiness, it leads to repentance and conversion, it is caring in its core, and it blesses and brings favor. Jesus read from Isaiah in His hometown of Nazareth at His synagogue, "That the blind see, that the deaf hear, that the lame walk, and that prisoners are released and a year of favor has come upon us." The Word of God set the pattern of redemption and atonement in His calling. He alone is the Messiah. He is the Good Shepherd who cares for His sheep and who lays down His life for them.

Listening to God involves not just our ears, but our eyes and emotions. We listen to God the way we listen to each other. God set this pattern of listening in our nature and He blesses it through the incarnation of His Son. As Jesus gets up to read from Isaiah, and before anything is said, we see Him standing there with the open scroll in His hand. We feel His presence as He holds the scroll. The eyes of everyone see Him as He cradles each one of us with the promise of God's healing and God's favor[60] (see Luke 4:16-23).

LORD I WANT TO FEEL YOUR LOVE

Many people in sacramental churches are skeptical of emotion. Exuberant faith and prayer are seen by some liturgical purists as distractions. I have heard some clergy say, "Let those charismatics go to their own churches, we don't need all this hugging and touching and raising hands. It is a distraction that keeps me from concentrating." When we look into the Scriptures, we find that Jesus prayed with feeling. He wept at the tomb of Lazarus. He didn't wear his feelings on his sleeve, but neither did he hide them. He got angry and he felt all our other human emotions. If we are going to listen to Jesus, we need to experience His feelings.

The human condition is ripe with emotion. A caring Christian is not driven by kinesthetic impulses, but is connected to meaning through them. Every encounter with Jesus in the Scriptures is packed with feelings. Just examine any text, like in John's Gospel when Nicodemus came to see Jesus by night. What emotions are revealed in the biblical narrative?[61] (See John 3:1-19). The fear of Nicodemus to meet Jesus in the daylight when others could see him was similar to John's community that was fearful to openly confess their belief in Christ for fear of persecution by the Jews or by Rome? Are there sources of conflict? Are there hardships and difficulties in the world today that cause us to be afraid? Jesus answers our fear with an invitation. The surprise is that we can be born again. Do you want to live in fear or live in the Spirit of God? Feelings matter to Jesus. He never retreats from emotions. He faces them and experiences them, and He does this by placing them in God's care. Divine providence is the belief that God will take care of you. It is not just a feeling, but it includes feelings of trust. If I am going to listen to God, it is essential that I trust in His Word.

My father and mother have lived the life of divine providence for years. Their story is captured in my father's book, *And That's Not All.* I hope to publish it someday soon. It tells of God's wonderful blessings in their life as they trusted that as they worked in His vineyard, Jesus would take care of their needs. As their oldest son, I shared this life with them. It is an experience that has trained me to feel God's presence through His provision and care.

God wants us to feel His love so that His grace will attach us to Him. He is not interested only in a cerebral relationship any more than you are. For example, it is not enough to tell my wife I love her. She has to be confirmed in its truth and trust by the emotional connection of touch and hugs and kisses, and so do I.

When I visit patients, I tr y to touch ever y one. I grasp a hand or touch the top of a hand or arm. I put my hand on a shoulder or forehead when I pray for them. Jesus touched those He healed, and they touched Him. [62]

Listening to God is letting Him touch my emotions and my vulnerabilities. The hospital is often a cold place—not only emotionally, but physically. They literally keep the temperature down to decrease infections. Patients are poked, stuck with needles, or worse. I offer a caring touch of Jesus that affirms hope. Christ's touch in my soul in contemplation blesses me in ways my intellect can't understand. My soul feels His love with His touch. My spirit hungers to feel His love and care more and more. Christ does not need dried fruit with all the juice and zest removed.[63] God wants us to be fruit that is full of life with emotions and dreams and hopes. His Word is inspiring, fascinating, full of possibilities, and is not dull and boring. Christians are to be alive and vibrant, not apathetic and aloof and disinterested.

We can find and feel our own heartbeat and pulse as evidence of our physical condition. If our heartbeat is too slow, we feel sluggish and tired. If our heartbeat is too rapid at rest, we pant and try to breathe. If our pulse is irregular and skips its normal beat and rhythm, we get pain in our chests. These are feelings that are produced when we have symptoms of a heart condition. The Church experiences the heartbeat of Jesus when we care for each other and intercede with Christ in prayer. The pulse of the Spirit is in the Body of Christ. It puts us in touch with our needs. We need to be taking our spiritual pulse often. Are we slow and sluggish in responding to an invitation to care for someone who needs a kind word or encouragement? Are we so preoccupied that we don't take the time to listen to our children or spouse? Are we so busy that we binge on the adrenalin of worldly success or fame or power? Do we live with a gnawing pain in our chest that says things are not right? I think the reason people today are afraid to feel is because they are reluctant to pray. Dialogue with God will move me to the heart of things and there I can feel His presence.

LORD I WANT TO SEE YOU!

When I was in fourth grade, our school had a vision test for all the children. I was promptly identified as a kid who needed glasses. I could hardly make out any of the sideway E's, or letters that didn't spell words. When my new glasses arrived and I put them on, suddenly my whole world changed. Colors became clearer. Trees had leaves, and to my surprise, the chalkboard in my class had writing on it. I had a revelation. If I can see, then I can learn more, and maybe get better grades.

Many of Jesus' miracles were healing of the blind.[64] Prayer opens us to see Jesus. I want to look at Him and see the world and myself through His eyes. The Scriptures are full of visual encounters with Jesus. We see Him moving from place to place. We see Him washing the apostles' feet.[65] We see Him teach, train, and send out the seventy-two disciples. Most of all, we see Jesus caring for people with love and truth.[66]

We have so many religious icons, paintings, art, and sculpture attempting to show not only what Christ looked like, but to engage us with His personality. The artist tries to communicate something about Christ more than just a fanciful likeness. When I was about eighteen years old, a priest friend of mine asked me to do a poster drawing of Christ for a class he was teaching. It was a kind of anti-drug, anti-corrupt world idea. I was in my room one night working on the poster. It was of Jesus, not on the cross, but trying to get through a wall of addictions that kept Him out of our hearts. He was desperately trying to get though to us. As I worked on it, the picture began to emerge so very easily that I was amazed. I did not have the ability then to draw a person with the proper facial and bodily proportions, and yet there they were. I began to sob because I not only was aware that Jesus was guiding my work, but that I had the wall of my own ego keeping Him out of my life.

Suddenly, I had an experience of Jesus as Lord that I did not see coming. It was not long after this experience that I was prayed over for the baptism of the Holy Spirit. Jesus communicated His desire to get through my defenses through the medium of visual representation. He wanted to enter into my dominate mode of communication.

Any time we meditate on Christ's life, we experience a new view into His love for us and our love for Him. Seeing moves us closer to the object of our attention. We learn lessons through sight. We remember through sight. We experience bonding through sight. We contemplate the world and its meaning through sight. Thomas had to see the wounds of Christ. He needed to touch and feel them and He had to hear the Word of Jesus dispelling his grief, sorrow, betrayal, and disbelief. Each sense helped him penetrate deeper into the meaning of Christ's sacrifice and atonement for his sins.[67]

I think that mystical union with God is His plan for all of us. Jesus wants to lead us to the Father in the Spirit. He moves us by communicating His love through our senses of seeing, hearing, and feeling. Classical mystical theology speaks of three major steps on the journey to union with Christ. Purgation, illumination, and union.[68]

Each one of these three developmental stages is experienced through seeing, feeling, and hearing. We don't always recognize what Jesus is trying to heal in us because we may have buried our pain, loss, hurt, and resentments by shutting down one or two of the channels (visual, auditory, and feeling) that God uses to communicate with us.

Purification is when God tries to open a channel of dialogue where the pain is great. We often resist His overtures. Sometimes an event like sickness or a loss of a job or some suffering begins to stretch our illusion of self-confidence or control. It can be a crisis of a transition through a stage of life, like menopause, mid-life, parenthood, or the empty nest. Usually it manifests itself with an inability to cope emotionally or spiritually to the stress of the situation. Life will cause the painful reality of our limitations and mortality to become obvious. When this happens, and it happens to everyone, we search for meaning and hope. It is here in the heart of the person that God begins to move us closer to His heart of caring. It takes hard introspective work to recognize that God is trying to break down the barriers we have erected to protect ourselves. We begin to rely less on our egos or natural abilities and to trust in His grace. God moves us into illumination. There is a release when God's love breaks through our protection and we see him when we were blind to our neighbor's plight or to Jesus' gift of salvation. Our hearts can be consumed with worldly desires that calcify our compassion for one another. A heart that is stony resists feeling God's grace and care.[69] We may have blocked His Word by changing the subject, or interrupted His sentiment of caring for our soul. We may have been so full of our own thoughts and works and words that we have had little inclination to listen for His words of compassion, tenderness, love, and caring. God wants us to experience His love, not out of desperation because of our human mortality, but from a heart illuminated and softened by His Holy Spirit. The experience of the Baptism in the Holy Spirit centers our attention on the person of Jesus Christ. We learn a new prayer, one that is revealed in the Spirit.

Once I was baptized in the Holy Spirit, I could hear Him calling me to serve the people of God as a priest. I began to see His works and experience them for myself. I could see His leading and guiding in my life. Once I was baptized in the Holy Spirit, I could feel His sweet anointing and His visitation in my heart. It is because of His grace that this gift has been given to me. I know that Jesus is working in my heart. He desires an open communication that is not driven by what I want to protect, but by His desire to care for and love me. There is inner work to be done in this stage as well. Once God has called us, we must learn to follow. The temptation is to give up when things get difficult. I have experienced hardships and sufferings from the people I have tried to serve. The religious hierarchy was the most difficult audience that Jesus encountered. It is difficult to forgive those who harm or hurt you. Lessons of service and faithfulness are hard to learn when there is suffering. Yet, slowly, through God's grace, we are shaped into the likeness of His Son.

Union with God happens in that place where our hearts are formed to be like His. Where we are attuned to His will. When we do the things He wants us to do in the way He wants them done, we, then, care for others as He cares for us and we depend on His grace all the time. I have not arrived at this place, but I have had glimpses of it.

Kathrine Kuhlman said in one of her revivals something like this. "People want to know, 'Have you seen visions of Jesus or been taken up to heaven?'" She said, "I am reminded of a story in the Old Testament about Joseph who was sold into slavery by his own brothers, and that eventually he made himself known to them after he had become a powerful man in Egypt. They returned to their father Israel with news that Joseph was alive. Now, Israel's reaction was one of disbelief until he saw the wagons full of grain, bread, and food that Joseph had sent. Israel believed that Joseph was alive, when he saw the wagons (Gen. 45ff)." Kuhlman went on to say, "I haven't had a vision of Jesus or been taken up to heaven in the Spirit," but she said, "I have seen the wagons! I know that Jesus is alive," Tears flowed down her face "I know He is alive because I have seen the wagons!"

When we are walking in union with God, we see the wagons. We see healings, miracles, signs, wonders, and we experience the transforming power of the Holy Spirit working with us and through us. We witness the wagons full of blessings, grace, and love. They are produced by the person who is the Living Sabbath.

The Old Testament sets aside a day of rest as holy to God. We are told that God rested from the work of creation and He wanted His people to enter into His rest.[70] We are to mirror back creation's response to this duet of reflection and repose. We find in the New Testament that Jesus is hardly at rest on the Sabbath.[71] When we enter into His rest, things happen. When we enter into His rest, we enter into His heart. We can be ourselves with Jesus. We can rest in Him because we don't have to meet worldly goals. We don't have to work ourselves into heart attacks or anesthetize our pain and pretend it doesn't hurt.

Sin takes a lot out of us. Often in the hospital, I see young people in their twenties or thirties who have so abused their bodies that you would think, by looking at them, that they are three times their age. A life of dissipation is exhausting. Jesus is the Sabbath rest in person. His care changes the way we relate to the world and to ourselves. It's not a mad crazy rush to prominence. It is an invitation to a life of prayer and caring for each other. Purgation is doing the work of God and following His laws because it is good to do so. People of spiritual importance have said so. We are better off when we follow His commands. Illumination is doing what we think God wants us to do. It includes study, spiritual discipline, and prayer. Union with God (The Unitive Way) is doing what God is doing. It's living in the Sabbath rest with Jesus in the Spirit. We enter into this way by relying on the gift of God's grace. Many people follow the politically powerful—the person of celebrity, the successful, or the intellectual guru who promises a pain free life. Our culture is full of false hope and messiahs who persuade people to accept the latest fad religion. They make promises that they cannot possibly deliver. Building an idol is easy and tempting. We can create a false god out of anyone or anything. It can happen so quickly that we don't even know we have done it. Just like the people of Israel in the desert when they said they didn't know how it happened. They just put this gold together in this fire and out popped this golden calf.[72]

Our culture believes in the magic of immediacy, technology, and a special knowledge that puts us above any so-called god. The attraction to the occult begins with creating an idol. It contains three subtle deceptions. Each one of the three temptations of Christ involve the senses of seeing, hearing, and feeling. The devil wants to turn them into channels of prideful self-protection and away from hearing and obeying the Father, trusting in His love, and being faithful to seeing the kingdom of God. The temptations of Christ describe the content of these assaults on the nature of God's care.[73] They are also our temptations because we are tempted the same way and through the same senses. The enemy recognized that Jesus was hungry. He told Jesus that there was no need to feel this way. Just make bread for yourself. No need to rely on the Word of God when He is silent and you are lonely. Put God's Word to the test. Make sure for yourself that it is true by throwing yourself down. God will catch you, won't He? Finally, look and see all the stuff that I can show you, to make your life pleasant. Fall down and worship the devil.

Jesus gives his response directly to the assault on the heart of God's care. "Man does not live by bread alone but by the Word of God." God will take care of me and I will hold onto His promises. "Do not put the Lord your God to the test." God's Word is not about proof. It's about belief and trust in God's care. "The Lord your God shall you worship and Him alone shall you serve." No idol can measure up to the living God who cares for me and whom I serve. Jesus enters into His and our humanity and becomes obedient to the God who cares. He is not the idol of comfort and pleasure. Jesus takes the mantle of dependency on God because He knows and loves God. Jesus accepts the sacrifice that is required to bring redemption to the world, and we are called by His grace to do the same. The apostles ask Jesus to teach them to pray. In Luke 11:2-5 (nrsv) He says, "When you pray, say: "Father, hallowed be your name. Your kingdom come. Give us each day our daily bread. And forgive us our sins, for we ourselves forgive everyone indebted to us. And do not bring us to the time of trial."

The elements of this prayer prepare our hearts to adopt the attitude of care that is essential to being a disciple. Jesus does not just talk and the Father listens. Rather, He enters into a dialog with God. He knows about listening as well as speaking. The prayer He gives us is like a prelude to prayer. It readies our hearts to listen to God by going down the list of things that infect our minds with concerns. Jesus understands our human preoccupations and cares for us by saying aloud those things that divide us so easily from God's heart of love.

The first step is to recognize to whom you are speaking and who is going to speak to you. God is holy and His name is the name above all other names. We begin this preparation for prayer by standing empty before God. He is the one whom we adore. He is the one we worship, and He alone is the King of the kingdom. Once we are in this place of recognition of God's love and care (holiness), then we can begin to accept His kingdom. We are not in charge. He is, and His kingdom will be established on His terms. If I believe that God is the planner, then I have to believe in His plan. If an architect comes up with a drawing for a new building, or if a military general comes up with a plan for battle, to accept the plan means to recognize the importance of the planner. If the president tells the general he doesn't like the plan, or if the contractor says to the architect that he doesn't like the design, they will have to get a different general or architect. Once we accept God's holiness, then we also identify His holiness in the plan of caring for each other in Christ. We ask for His kingdom to come in us. His purposes are to be our purposes—His plans to be our plans.

"Give us each day our daily bread." attaches us to the truth that God cares for us and provides for us each day. We recognize His provision for our needs and sustenance. To enter into the world of God's care we accept the gift of His divine providence. Many of Jesus' teachings revolve around trusting that God will take care of us and that we can trust Him. We are invited to lay aside our temptation to provide for ourselves and to set our own course in self provision. As disciples we must articulate dependence on God not just for our physical needs but for our spiritual needs as well. Bread refers not just to food, but to community, fellowship, relationships, family, and emotional and spiritual intimacy. God's provision extends to the bread of human society and familial bonds. We are to trust these relationships into God's hands for His divine care. We are to care for each other as God cares for us in Christ.

The next step is forgiveness. It is a pointless exercise to progress to this point and have a grievance against anyone. I cannot move into dialog with God if my mind and heart are taken up with bitterness against my brother or sister. Reconciliation is the heart of the Gospel. Jesus came to extend this forgiveness to everyone. I have the same amount of forgiveness in my heart as I am willing to extend forgiveness to someone who hurts, disappoints, or rejects me. Each one of these steps is built on God's care and love. I have spoken in Chapter 2 about how to do the ministry of reconciliation and absolution. I refer you back to that chapter.

Finally, we have saved the best for last. It has saved us from the time of trial. If you are moving into discipleship, you know what this means. It is to be treated in the same way Jesus was treated. He was well aware that His words and deeds would ruffle the feathers of the established religious elite. Over and again He prepared the apostles for the day that was coming when He would be delivered to evil men. There were times when people wanted to throw Him off a hill or stone Him or plot some other way of getting rid of Him. He thwarted every one of their little dramas. Often, He just walked right past them and went on His way. If we are His disciples, we have to place our future in God's hands. Nothing we may face can separate us from the love and care of the Father.

We have to place the future of our families, church, society, and friends in the benevolent care of God. We may have to face a time of trial, but we don't have to face it alone, for the Holy Spirit will guide us in what to say if that day comes. We are facing a culture that is increasingly resistant to the Gospel. It is not difficult to see the conflict that is brewing for those committed to Jesus Christ. In this time and in the future we must trust God's Word shown to us through Christ.

Now I am ready to listen. Now I am open to hearing God's voice in my soul. We are used to praying the "Our Father" quickly and without much reflection—almost out of habit. We should be using it as a tool to prepare us to dialogue with God through His heart of love. Each step draws us deeper into His care. With each sentiment, our hearts mirror a common rhythm of God's covenant with us through Jesus Christ. Now, let's be quiet and listen to what God has to say to our minds and hearts. (Pause) You may add this short meditation on the Sacred Heart of Jesus after the "Our Father."

A MEDITATION ON THE SACRED HEART OF JESUS

The first heartbeat of Jesus began just as we did in the womb of expectation. The Old Testament promise had been made real. With each beat of His heart, the world changed as the day of God's kingdom grew closer. He burst upon the waters of our humanity giving birth to the fulfillment of God's Word. The Word made flesh, full of grace and truth. His heart is full of tenderness and compassion. It beats with the rhythm of angelic hosts, of creation, of self sacrifice, of love and care. He willingly took his heart to Calvary for you and me. There, he experienced trauma and shock, violence and pain, sin and rejection, betrayal and abandonment. And when the cup was empty, when the work of redemption was finished, his heart beat one last time… and ruptured… and broke… and stopped. Jesus cried out with a loud voice, and died. His blood was separated into water and plasma which filled the sack around His heart and compressed it tightly. A spear pierced it and out poured water and blood.[74] In that moment, salvation washed over us like a flood. It drenched us in baptism. It swallowed up death and sin forever. Now, His heart beats with the rhythm of redemption. Now it beats with the power of the resurrection. Now He shares it with you and me. Now we pray with His heart in the Spirit. Now you and I care for one another with His heart that will never stop. Now His heart beats forever and we live.

PLEASE WRITE DOWN YOUR RESPONSES TO THE MEDITATION

What did you hear as you read the words in the meditation aloud? As you listen to Him now, what is He saying to you?

_____

_____

_____

_____

What did you feel as the meditation touched your heart? What emotion is God's presence raising inside you right now?

_____

_____

_____

_____

What vision of God's heart do you see at work in you? Describe what you see as you meditate on God's heart of love.

_____

_____

_____

_____

Write your own prayer below as a response to what you have heard, felt, or seen as you meditate on the sacred heart of Jesus

_____

_____

_____

_____

NOTES AND REFLECTIONS

AT THE GATE

It's all about whose side you're on.

Am I the one who decides who comes in or staysout?

Am I the one who wishes to go across that frontier or who wishes to remain whereI am?

A gate can remainclosed or open.

It swingsboth ways.

It comes with a choice and sodoes He.

JESUS SAYS: I AM THE GATE

Lord Jesus, let me open my heart to You. Let me say "yes" to Your invitation to come into Your presence.

This gate is not an obstacle, it offers a choice. He says, "Come in." So must I.

(A Place for Your Reflection and Prayer)

_____
_____
_____
_____
_____
_____
_____
_____
_____
_____
_____
_____
_____
_____
_____
_____
_____
_____
_____
_____
_____
_____
_____
_____

CHAPTER 6

THE TRINITY AND UNITY IN THE HEART OF CHRIST, "THE BRIDE AND THE *BRIDEGROOM*"

I WAS VERY sick with asthma as a little child, and I spent a lot of time in the hospital under an oxygen tent. In those days, the hospital medical staff saw parents as an impediment to recovery. They strictly adhered to the rule that every parent had to be out of the hospital by 8:00 p.m. I was a small sick kid and I didn't understand why my father and mother had to leave me. Well, my dad would often sneak back in and stay with me even though it was against hospital policy. I knew his footsteps and I felt comfort and love as he quietly found a chair next to me.

Years later, I was in the seminary just about halfway through my studies, but I still had a long way to go to ordination. I felt lonely; many of my good friends had gone home. I wondered if maybe my calling was only a dream. I felt doubt and confusion.

One night, around midnight, I was fretting and half asleep when I heard those footsteps. I knew it was my father! I remembered his walk. I felt his care and love coming towards me. The Lord had told him in prayer that I needed to see him. He drove all the way from Arizona to California that night. Like my father's ministry to me, God's love is communicated in ways that have echoed through 2,000 years of history. We hear Jesus stepping with us. We feel His familiar presence. He responds to our needs and pain. He cares for us and shepherds us to that day when He will come again and retrieve his bride the Church.[76] We will be in that everlasting Jerusalem full of love and glory.

THE HOLY TRINITY

The voice of the Father in Mark1:11 says that Jesus is His own dear Son and that God is pleased with Him. This is not selfsatisfaction, or only recognition of the Father's endowment of trust in His calling. Rather, it witnesses for us the unique character of God's self-donation in the act of redemption. The sacrifice of Jesus is the only sacrifice that could be pleasing to God because it comes from His altar to us. In the Old Covenant we offered God the gifts that represented humanities sustenance: sheep, bulls, and animals for sacrifice. However, they always ended up short of the mark because they were salted, not just with our best intentions, but with our sins. The gift of our redemption comes from a loving and caring God who is perfectly both God and man. At the Baptism of Jesus we see the full manifestation of the Trinity for the first time. We hear the voice of the Father. We see the Holy Spirit coming down upon Him, and we feel the love of the "son of man" who will take away the sins of the whole world. We have the three persons who are one God. They share a unity of purpose. They are a family intimately bonded with a relationship to each other that is dynamic, creative, holy, loving, and perfect. We have no direct knowledge of God's nature except through revelation. Jesus, in John 6:46-53, reveals the love of the Father. He has come so that the Father's love would be mirrored in His love for us. Jesus shows us the Father by caring for us— by giving us the new manna of His body and blood, and through His Word and works of obedience to the will of the Father.

LIVING IN THE MYSTERY OF THE TRINITY

I live in Arizona and I have been to the Grand Canyon many times. I have observed it throughout the day and at different seasons of the year. I have even had the opportunity to fly over it in a small plane. I have studied its geology and I have become acquainted with how science has given us a greater appreciation of its history and creation. When I bring a visitor to see it for the first time, I still find myself in awe of this magnificent Wonder of the World. I still find myself aware of the incredible mystery that the Canyon leaves in my senses and in my soul. Great art like the Sistine Chapel or the Mona Lisa create a place of mystery within our hearts. There is in mystery a revealed truth that life is not quite defined by our mind's understanding or grasped by science or described by observations or hypothesis. The frequency of mystery is abundant. In the hospital I see it from when a baby is born to when a person is in need of God's touch.

The mystery of the Trinity is not a way to avoid talking about a complex and difficult concept. The mystery of the Holy Trinity is our way of life. Christians are people who accept mystery even as we seek to learn more about it. We are not trying to dislodge it from reality. We are committed to celebrating mystery because it is present everywhere. Disciples seek out mystery, and hold up its creative reality. Once we accept the mystery of the Trinity, we can be more in touch with the mystery of God's presence in everyone and in the world around us. The journey of the Church in the Spirit, mirrors the relationship of the Trinity. We experience the divine guidance of the Holy Spirit. The bond of love between the Father and the Son manifests itself in our experience. In the Spirit, we have seen "the wagons." We have heard His familiar footsteps and we have felt the love of the Holy Spirit.

Over time these experiences of mystery have formed representational traditions of theology. The early church first identified them as: Word, Sacrament, and Spirit. Time and history have reshaped them. Today we define them as evangelical, Catholic, and charismatic. These three traditions are representational systems that describe the experience of God's mystery. They are like channels of communication. The one we use the most seems best to us because it represents our world view and beliefs. Our challenge is to build a new unity in the church using all three.

I am aware that the history of Christianity and its denominational teachings and conflicts are not easily disentangled. They are complex and deeply rooted in our past. I am not naive or arrogant to think that I have all the answers to Christianity's disunity. I realize I am making some theological generalizations. My purpose is to build a process or way forward to a deeper dialogue. We need to harness a language of caring that mirrors the attitudes of the early church. Reformed theology has focused on the Word of God and the Holy Scriptures as the revealed truth of God's salvation and grace. We are saved by accepting Jesus into our hearts and through believing in Him and His Word.

Catholics see God's grace through symbols—the sacraments, prayer, and liturgy. Charismatics are identified with the action of the Holy Spirit and the gifts of the Spirit. This belief is the Pentecostal experience of salvation in Christ and the manifestation of His Holy Spirit. Evangelicals are Wordoriented and more auditory. Catholic is sacramental and focuses on visual representations of the Gospel. Charismatic is experiential and more connected to feelings. Jesus reveals His love for the Church through all three channels. He is working with us to open up the theological pathways we may have closed down. We need to admit our painful past of hurt and suffering that has been caused by our historical, theological, and political conflicts. Moving from the past will mean an engagement outside our particular theological vocabulary.

The Anglican Mission in the Americas is the first group that has talked about these three streams moving together as a river. So, how do we bring the ecclesiology of unity forward? I understand that we will meet resistance to this paradigm's emergence.

I recently had a conversation with a fellow priest about the Eucharist. He was coming from a more evangelical, Wordoriented theological and personal understanding of sacrament. During our conversation, I became aware of how differently we understood and explained the faith. I was talking in a visual and Catholic channel, and he was coming from an Evangelical and hearing stream of belief. We were talking past and over each other. Somehow we ended up on different sides of the fence that we had created. We were both right and both wrong at the same time.

The Anglican Church has a long history of subdividing itself by defending its rubrics in the Book of Common Prayer: which version is the best, the 1928 or the 1979, or other versions. We can argue about anything and celebrate that we have the inside track on the true Gospel. Historically and theologically, we have built as many bridges to unity as we have torn down. If we are going to change and produce a river of Living Water,[76] it will have to be centered in the heart of Jesus. Its headwaters are in pastoral care. The work of Unity in the Spirit is not an outcome like a goal. It is the result of residing in the caring heart of Jesus. It is faithfully recognizing the Holy Trinity as the pattern for unity. It is living in the mystery of the Kingdom of God, and the benefits of God's grace.

Serving the needs of the poor, visiting the sick, and caring for one another produces unity. Pastoral care is the vanguard of unity because this ministry is centered in the heart of God's loving care. We do not do theology and then care. We care, and from that experience of mystery, we do theology.

In the late 1960's there was a movement that caught fire called the Charismatic Renewal. It came to the Catholic Church from the influence of the Pentecostal churches, and began at Notre Dame University. After a time, it got to Phoenix, Arizona. I was just finishing Catholic high school when one day my father asked me to go with him to a prayer meeting. I said I would, and off we went.

Well, it was the craziest thing I had ever seen. I was not prepared for this praying in tongues stuff. I told my dad after the meeting, "You should never go back there." Not only did he go back, but soon he was praying in tongues and so was my mother. They started having a prayer meeting in our home. Though I was hesitant at first, I slowly started attending, and then at one meeting I asked Jesus into my heart and received the baptism in the Spirit. I found myself praying in tongues.

The Charismatic Renewal is part of my spiritual history. I brought it with me to the seminary, and in those days, that was not easy. I have kept that experience alive in my personal life of prayer to this day. The Renewal, in my opinion, has somewhat died down, but its influence has not. Throughout the 70's, 80's, and 90's many people who were baptized in the Spirit were led into other churches. Catholics went to Evangelical churches. Pentecostals to Catholic churches. Evangelicals went to Pentecostal or Catholic churches. The renewal has not ended. It has expanded across the board to include the entire church. The Holy Spirit has leavened the bread of fellowship and caring among all Christ's family. The work of unity is being done in the Spirit at the grassroots level.

The Charismatic renewal was not just about starting prayer meetings or having retreats or seminars or conventions. It was and is about building unity in the household of God. Today, I see the movement of the Holy Spirit continuing to break down hardened attitudes that keep us in theological camps. When we center our attention on the Heart of Christ's caring in the Spirit, unity is always the result.

One of the most important gifts to the Church which we need to share is affirmation. Rather than counting on our differences to polarize us, we need to affirm the gifts of caring in each other. For too long we have guarded our religious territory. For too long we have hoarded our gifts for our own goals and needs. For too long we have placed the Gospel between us like a wall. The gospel, however, is a bridge to the heart of God's caring. Because of the wall we have built, the world does not believe in the possibility of unity in Christ's Body. The effect has been that our disunity mimics the world's fascination with power. The result is that when we speak, the world does not care to listen because we act toward each other just as those in any other worldly institution. When that happens, we compromise the meaning of the mystery of God's redemption.

THE INNER HEALING OF THE BRIDE OF CHRIST

Some time ago I was training and coaching a couple in active listening. I tell couples that I am not a counselor, but a trainer. I hope to give them skills to listen to their spouse, and from there, they can begin to solve their own problems. I became aware during our session that some of their issues were old reenacted childhood pains. They were reactions from the past that had emerged from the subconscious. The couple could hear the old emotional wounds, but did not know what to do about them. Sometimes the spouse, without their understanding, became the receiver of the pain of past hurt or loss or abandonment. At such moments of transference, I began to train couples to ask Jesus to heal the memories that needed His forgiveness and healing touch. Dorothy and I have done inner healing with each other throughout our thirty-year marriage. The experience has drawn us closer together.

If the three streams of charismatic, Catholic, and evangelical to move together, it will take not just communication, but inner healing. We have a lot to get over—years of religious conflict between denominations. We have excommunications, historical mistrust of each other, and attitudes that keep us apart. The pain of our history and disunity will require a concerted effort of prayer to the bridegroom. The church must learn to accept anew the patterns of unity in Christ. Just as in marriage, old scripts or pain from the past will emerge. It is in such moments of transference that a new direction for healing and reconciliation can develop.

There are several forces that are plunging the church into this mystery of inner healing:

- First, the most powerful force is persecution. When persecution comes, Christians, no matter what denomination they might be, band together. Throughout the world, persecution for the sake of the gospel is at an all-time high.

- Second, the church has to articulate a moral theology that speaks to the world about ethical behavior because modern culture opposes religion and its teachings. The church needs to speak to societal confusion about abortion, euthanasia, homosexual marriage, and other issues.

- Third, the power of unity in the Spirit is drawing us together in common patterns of worship and liturgy. We need to feel a sense of belonging to the gospel and to each other.

- Fourth, our nation's population is slowly aging. Christian caregiving is a natural ministry that brings us together in serving the needs of Christ's body.

These four realities are opportunities for a new movement of God to reshape the future church. Under the pressure of persecution, secular modern culture, aging populations, and the need for bonding and belonging, the church can propel its way forward from the past. It will open us up to the possibilities for the coming New Jerusalem and with it the Bridegroom. Its commonalities are these:

1. An assiduous reading of the Holy Scriptures, including Bible studies and gospel application for pastoral and theological reflection.

2. A hunger for Eucharistic celebration—liturgical prayer along with charismatic gifts and worship.

3. A common moral stance supporting the dignity of human life that is opposed to the culture of death, abortion, and euthanasia.

4. An agreement on the foundational dogma of the Holy trinity, the two natures of Christ, and the meaning of grace.

5. A biblical view of sexual ethics, marriage, and family.

6. A pastoral and caring direction with a focus on the proclamation of Gospel.

7. A basic ecclesiology of caring for each other as the body of Christ,

8. Leadership models that are based on servant authority and a calling from God as well as a calling from the community to ordained service.

9. Supportive care for the family as the building block of the faith community.

10. The importance of intercessory prayer for the Church and the world, personal prayer, and corporate prayer.

12. The importance for ongoing education and training in the faith. Participation with other denominations in ministry and worship.

These essential characteristics have emerged as patterns arising from our unity in the Spirit. It has started, and it is growing. All around us people are being led by the Spirit into the ministry of caring. I am well aware that there is resistance to these developments and that many in the church are not prepared to make this leap. I am also aware of the effects of a long history of disunity and rehearsed theological conflicts. I do not minimize the difficulties ahead, but I believe "the day" is coming. And I believe Jesus is the only one who can establish this "new day." He is the one who can come into the upper room of our disunity and bring peace. I pray that this day will come soon. What will be the signs? How can we tell that this day is approaching? We will need a new affirmation of our calling as this inner healing of the Church moves forward?

Affirmation, the Sign of Inner Healing in the Church

It is a sad reality that clergy are rarely affirmed. Oh, once in a while someone says, "That was a good sermon, pastor," or, "You made a good teaching or presentation." Outside of some special anniversary or big occasion such as ordination, affirmation is a dish seldom tasted by the clergy. It is such a rare occurrence that it bleeds over into our relationships with each other. Clergy meetings can consist of pietistic posturing and theological and intellectual defenses that have no outcomes, only long discussions—a kind of theological impotence. We can hold meetings that are superficial, tiring, and boring. We don't affirm each other. What would it be like if every Sunday was an affirmation Sunday? After all, isn't that what happened to us in Christ's resurrection. God affirmed us all by making us His children. How blessed we are in being disciples and parts of Christ's body; how blessed we are by the ministry of the pastor or priest and church leaders.

I have served mostly in small churches. In my last parish, it was uncanny how after I had given what I thought was a moving homily, one of my parishioners, after mass, would send me a zinger such as: "Why did you forget the Gloria?" Or, "Why did you say the liturgy so fast?" Or some other minor rubrical infraction. I began to measure my sermons by how many zingers I got after church. One zinger was a good sermon. Two zingers was really a great sermon. And three zingers meant that I had ascended to the level of the angelic hosts.

I know that all these zingers are cries for help. Still, sometimes the lack of affirmation builds into hopelessness and defeat. The absence of affirmation among clergy leads to a kind of pervasive mediocrity. We just try to get through to the next thing, the next program, or meeting. The zeal of the young creative pastor is viewed as naïve. Just give him time and the effect of the zinger equation will level the playing field and bring him down to earth.

The death of affirmation destroys unity. It is during our clergy gatherings that we feel the effects of disunity the most. We can be skilled champions of our own theological positions and capable of zingers on a Machiavellian scale. The possible result might be that we could become like a cursed fig tree.[77] Christ's priestly prayer in John's Gospel invites us into the place where Jesus abides in unity.[78] He equates this unity to the love between Him and the Father, and He invites us to join them.

As I discussed earlier, the baptism of Jesus in the Gospels is the affirmation of the Holy Spirit and the Father upon Jesus. The story begins the Gospel of Mark and is early in the other gospels because it is so important. We get to hear the voice of heaven resonate with the sound of redemption. "You are my Son, the Beloved; with you I am well pleased."[79] It is spoken to Jesus so that we all hear the voice of the Father. We all see the Spirit come down upon Him and we feel God's affirming love swirl the water of baptism. Now those words are spoken to us. "You are my Son [or daughter], the Beloved; with you I am well pleased."[80] God affirms us in Christ. He affirms the Church to be His bride bejeweled with virtue, robed in the sacrifice of martyrs, aglow in the gifts of the Spirit, radiant in holiness, and adorned with the witness of love and service to others.[81] The greatest sign of the inner healing of the church is the affirmation of the ministry of laity and clergy. God's favor rests on us. That means His holiness affirms our calling.

How many of us believe that we are holy? Christians are far more likely to be aware of their sinfulness than their holiness in Christ. Yet, the introductions of many of Paul's letters begin "To all the saints in … (add your own town or city)."[82] We know that through the death and resurrection of Jesus, God saves his creation, and in doing so, He affirms its worth and holiness. Worship is the response we make through grace to God's affirmation in Christ. How much more can God do? He brings us into His family and consecrates us to His service. If the Church is going to be a caring place, it must also be an affirming place. God's affirmation is not a license to do what we want for ourselves. God continues to have boundaries. He draws us into conversion. [83] He is not about to water down the Word so that everyone will feel included.[84] He is all about making a decision, accepting His Father's invitation to change and follow Him. He affirms us by giving us this choice. He pushes the gift of redemption back into our hands. Do we believe God's affirmation?

Do we accept the treasure he puts in our soul? In the affirmation that, "Nothing can separate us from God's love."[85] Saint Paul tells us to hold on to the prize we have been given. Jesus says The Kingdom of God is the pearl of great price because He is eternal life.[86]

My father loves to tell the story about his first lesson of unity from his father. When he was a youngster, he used to help his dad cut hay in a field that was owned by the local Protestant church. My grandparents used to feed their animals with what they harvested from this field. One day they were working. It was hot and they had no water. My dad was really thirsty, so his father told him that he knew of a place where there was cool water. He led him down to the Protestant church. Now in those days, it was a mortal sin to go into a Protestant church. At first, my father was resistant, but grandfather reassured him that it was okay. Sure enough, they found a drinking fountain that had cool water to quench their thirst and revive them. My grandfather told my dad this simple truth. "You see, Protestant water tastes just like Catholic water." Once we have tasted the water of unity we cannot help but desire it more and more. Once the Church has experienced the affirmation in the Spirit that comes from unity, it must witness to the Spirit's lifegiving power. Once we have tasted the living water of caring for the body of Christ, we are revived in unity.[87] Our spirits are nurtured in love in the waters of baptism and the Church is birthed and reborn in hope.

Jesus tells us in Mark 4:21 "Is a lamp brought in to be put under the bushel basket, or under the bed, and not on the lampstand?"[88] Light in a dark room does two important things. First, it lets us see where we are. When I stay in a strange place, such as a hotel, I need a light to locate where I am in relationship to other things. If I don't have light, I risk running into things and falling. Second, light provides a safe way to find the proper direction to my destination. When I am in the dark and cannot see, I am confused. I get easily disoriented and so I may feel insecure and lost.

Jesus is the light of the world.[89] He has come to dispel darkness. He wants us to know where we are and to see where we are going. God does not want us stumbling into confusion, doubt, and fear. He reveals His love by caring for us, even to the point of going to the cross and dying.

He points us in the proper direction through His Holy Spirit and the Spirit leads us into unity.

Many people are attracted to the light in the same way bugs swarm around the front porch light that I leave on all night for security. People fly to the light. They sometimes attend church and practice the religious rituals that may include every kind of leisure activity.

Jesus, however, calls us into a deeper relationship. He wants us to appropriate the light and not just be attracted to it. We are affirmed by shining out to the world and by lighting the way for others to see where they are and where they are going. The witness of caring in the heart of Christ is leading us to unity in the Spirit; and it is happening all over the world right now!

Here is a short description of "THE COMMUNICATION OF GRACE" Followed by a page for your reflection.

THE COMMUNICATION OF GRACE

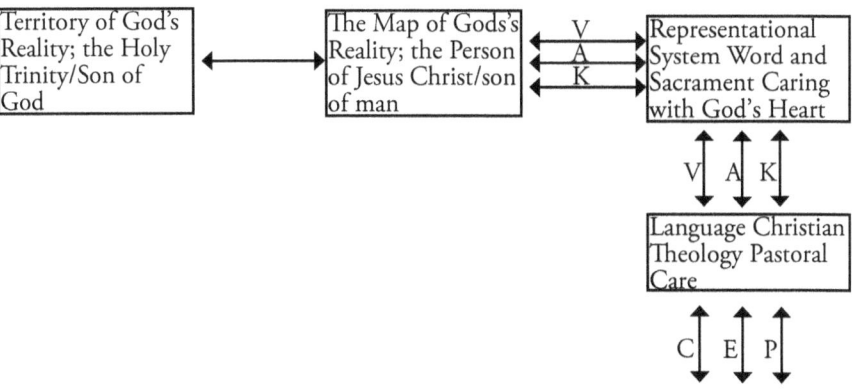

Linguistic Theological Systems		
Visual Catholic	Auditory Evangelical	Kinesthetic Pentecostal
Liturgy	Sermons	Praying in the Spirit
Prayer books	No decorations	Holding hands
Incense	Simple attire	Slain in the Spirit
Icons	Baptism by immersion	Prayer meetings
Seasonal colors	Altar calls	Raising up hands
Arts	Membership	Dancing in the Spirit
Architecture	Personal acceptance of Jesus	Prayer for Healing and
Sacraments	as Lord and savior	Deliverance

This is not a complete list and each community has music that fits the dominance whether it is visual, such as, "My Faith Looks up to Thee," or if it is auditory as in, "I Love to Tell the Story." Or perhaps it is kinesthetic, "Spirit of the Living God Fall Afresh on Me." The list is not exclusive. We can use any of these three channels of grace—visual, auditory, or kinesthetic— but we tend to use one more than the other two. We tend to resist using a dominant theological pattern that does not match up with our own representational system of communication. The material that forms the basis for the model comes from LEAD PLUS and their training manual, *Skills for Listening and Caring Ministries.*75

Please write a short reflection on where you're church may fit in one of these three categories—Visual Catholic,—Auditory Evangelical,— Kinesthetic Pentecostal.

Which is your dominant theological language? Is it the same dominant language that your church uses?

NOTES

LIGHTHOUSE

I see the Light!
In the Darkness
In the silent moments
Of fear.

I see the Light!
Atop the Hill
Shouting safety,
Safe harbor,
Patience.

I see the Light!
There is someone there
Someone ready to help
Someone looking, watching,
Caring, ready.
You, Oh Lord Jesus!

CHAPTER 7

THE CALL AND MINISTRY
TO PASTORAL CARE

THE CALL AND ministry of pastoral care comes from the mystery of the love of the Father. It is centered in the heart of Jesus Christ who cares for us, and it is expressed to us through the gifts of the Holy Spirit. Pastoral care mirrors the care Jesus gives to each of us. It is a calling through our baptism to minister to one another as Jesus ministers to us. Jesus says in John 15:15ff, that we are His friends, we know what to do. We know our calling. We do what Jesus does because we are His friends. Servants have to guess what the master wants because he does not confide in them. They find out about the will of the master after the fact. He tells them what to do. The master has the responsibility for the plans and their execution. The servant is not in on these details. Servants are not given any information other than what their job requires. However, in our case, a friend is in on the ground floor of planning. Because we are friends we are included in the process of decision making and we are consulted about plans and outcomes. Friendship with God is a relationship of mutual accountability. The Holy Spirit brings this new relationship of mutuality. Our partnership with God's plan of redemption in Christ, and our calling to the ministry of care invite us to experience the heart of Christ's grace— grace that rescues a person from the sea of sin, pain, sorrow, and death, and brings us into the abundant life as God's sons and daughters.

The seminary I attended was twelve miles from the ocean. I wanted to become a more proficient swimmer, so I decided to take a senior lifesaving class from one of my friends at school. He was certified by the State of California to teach and train people to be lifesavers. The course included CPR and water rescue training. Our seminary had a wonderful swimming pool. So twice a week we met and he taught me the art of rescuing a drowning person. The lessons that I learned from him have served me well in pastoral care. I learned from him that a rescuer must be observant. The same is true for a pastoral caregiver or chaplain. I am not talking about a detached kind of observation that is unsympathetic, aloof, and unengaged. The rescuer must be observing the situation with the intention of helping the person. The chaplain must also recognize the patient's condition. Is the patient awake? Are they hooked up to a variety of machines? What is their affect and emotional readiness to talk? Are they restrained? Are they free to move around? Are they on oxygen? Are they responsive or nonresponsive to my approach? Is there anyone with them? Are there pictures, cards, or flowers in the room? What do you see? What is the plight of the person?

Water rescue also requires a realistic assessment of the situation. Is the person in danger? Are they sinking to the bottom of the pool? Are they close to the edge? Is there anything I can throw them that they can grab onto while they float and are pulled in? How scared are they? Are they just tired or are they thrashing about in a panic? Jesus observed the situation around Him. He saw the boy tormented by a demon throw himself into the fire and roll around in the ashes.[90] He even asks the question, "How long has this been going on?" Jesus observed who put their money into the treasury for show and who gave out of her need.[91] He responded to the pastoral situation by being present to it. Even when He was pressed by a mob to make a decision about a woman caught in adultery, He waited and observed and felt the self-righteous demands for blood from the crowd. He never lost sight of his purpose as He wrote on the ground in front of them.[92]

Sometimes, after a brief moment of observation, it becomes apparent that the person is in real trouble. If there is nothing available to throw them, to rescue them you are going to have to get wet. Rescuing a person may mean that you have to place yourself in the same danger they are in. It is going to take a skill set that allows you to intervene without being drowned yourself. You have to realize that a person who is sinking will be in a panic. They will try to climb over you to get air and breathe. They will use you as flotation device even if it means drowning you in the process. The rescuer needs to know about this protection and not underestimate its power and potential danger. He must even be able to use this force of pain and fear to his advantage in rescuing the person. There are several things a rescuer must do to succeed. He needs to communicate to the person that help has arrived and it's going to be okay. He needs to say loudly that the person is going to have to follow his instructions. He needs to keep a distance between them so that the person struggling cannot grab at him as he approaches.

Pastoral caregivers need to use their active listening skills as they approach the patient. These skills include: story listening, neuro-linguistics, life commandment listening, creative questions, paraphrasing, perception checking, and other skills to build safety and rapport. Active Listening enables the person to begin the process of self-disclosure. The chaplain who uses these skills along with prayer and the guidance of the Holy Spirit will easily get to the point of pain of past hurt and present loss or present joy.

There are two parts of the actual rescue. The first step happens when the rescuer goes under water and swims beneath the person, then putting their hands on the person's hips, they push them up out of the water. This allows the drowning person to get a good breath of air and it also provides a sense of security. The second step is that rescuer, from underneath, slides the victim onto his or her back and begins to carry them in a cross-chest carry. The rescuer swims them to shore using sidestrokes and scissor kicks. Hopefully, the rescuer won't have to use any escape techniques to fend them off if they have somehow grabbed the rescuer around the neck or arms.

There are several more parallels about pastoral care that we can draw from this metaphor. We use active listening skills and the Spirit helps us become aware of the nature and intensity of the patient's pain. We call this the "aha" moment. When this happens, the caregiver realizes they are on holy ground. The patient has let us into their grief and loss, fear or pain, and for a time we are buoying them up. We give them the respite they need to breathe and express the pain that is drowning them. We then carry them to Jesus.

We have the wonderful story in Mark's Gospel about the paralyzed man who is let down through a hole in the roof that his friends made, so that Jesus can heal him (Mark 2:1ff). This is the moment of prayer. This is the time to meet the Lord who invites us into a relationship of safety and love. The good pastoral caregiver carries the tired and worn out person to the One who heals, frees, and forgives. It is not our job to supervise this meeting or make sure the outcome is the one we want. Jesus is quite capable of carrying on His own communication with the person. We are not the doctor. We only tend to the wounds so that Christ can do the healing.

Many people, who think of themselves as pastoral caregivers, rely on themselves to save the person. Believe me, we are not the Savior. We are not up to the task nor have we been given that authority. God has given the ability to save to His Son, and He has secured salvation by His death on the cross and His resurrection. We may help in the rescue, but it is Jesus alone who saves. He saved us from sin and death. When the waters were going to swallow us up forever, Christ came to deliver us. I think that is why so much of Jesus' ministry happened around the water. He frees a man from demons and possessed pigs drown themselves in the sea.[93] He gives the new law— the Beatitudes—next to the sea. He saves the apostles when their boat is about to sink. He walks on the water.[94] He is the lifeguard of our soul, and he will not let us drown.

Rescue has a negative connotation today with regard to pastoral care. Many think it is unacceptable to help someone when they should help themselves. The prevailing opinion is that we should not cross the boundary of a person's choice to drown if he or she wants to. What it often means is, "Let's avoid the danger or bad feelings if we fail. Let's excuse ourselves from helping, it's too difficult." This is not a biblical view of pastoral care. The pastoral caregiver has been saved by Christ. He has benefited from the ministry of someone who rescued him. He has his own redemption in Christ and experience of gratitude to God. They have received the same care that they now offer to someone else. The heart of God's salvation in Christ Jesus is that when I was drowning, God cared for me and saved me. We need to be aware and ready when an opportunity presents itself to rescue someone.

The pastoral caregiver must be prepared, like a lifeguard, and know how to respond if he should get grabbed and pulled under water. Small groups of committed Christians that meet regularly are essential to support each other in the ministry of care. The participants can review their listening skills, discuss their own issues and care needs, encourage each other, and affirm one another. Most importantly, they should pray for each other. Every one in the community can benefit from the training, practice, and participation.

The incarnation is all about God's loving saving grace. Jesus, by becoming man, gets into the water of our humanity with the intention and goal of saving us. Jesus is Emmanuel, "God with us" not to dazzle us with godlike tricks and slight of hand, but to save us, heal us, and bring us safely into His kingdom. One night Dorothy and I were preparing some peaches we had been given for a pie. We were both at the sink in the kitchen working on this little treasure when someone drove into our driveway. I heard a lot of noise outside and I ran out to investigate. I went toward the car that had its lights on and a man came around from the back of the car in hysterics. He was holding a little bundle and gave it to me. It was a baby and obviously something was very wrong with it. I could see a woman in the front seat who seemed to be in shock. It was dark, so I took the child and bent down as close as I could to the headlights. By this time, my wife was outside wanting to know what was going on. I told her to call 9-1-1, but I didn't tell her why.

I had all my attention on the child. I could see it was not breathing. I remembered my training, even though it had been many years ago, and I immediately tilted the babies head back and put my finger in its mouth to make sure that the airway was open. It still was not moving or responding. So I bent over and put my mouth over its mouth and nose and gave it a short little breath. It began to move a little and to whimper slightly. Just then the paramedics arrived. My wife had figured out that it was a child in trouble and had been able to answer the dispatcher's questions about the nature of the emergency. They took the child from me and brought it into our house, put a backboard on our couch and laid the baby on it. They then provided the needed care. By this time, I could tell that it was a little boy. The mother and father were being interviewed by the paramedics. The EMTs were in touch with a large hospital close by and it was likely that the child, who had a high temperature, had probably had a seizure. Once they had oxygen going and IV fluids running, they picked up the child and their equipment and went out the door to the hospital. It was so weird to be suddenly alone after all that had happened. I looked at Dorothy and said, "So, would you like to watch some TV?" We just laughed.

Being in a pastoral care moment is often difficult to describe to someone who does not share the experience. When God is doing what He does, we move from rescuer to observer. We have to be ready emotionally and spiritually to move with the person into closure and allow Jesus to claim the victory for saving the person. It has to always be about His work of salvation, not ours. Here again, it is important to have a group of Christians in your community that can help you debrief the experience.

In the story I just told, the father was too distraught to be of any help. Pain causes a person to become panic stricken and disoriented. Pastoral care means to be willing to become involved at the point of pain and to enter into the situation. The story also reveals the importance of training. Pastoral caregivers need to be trained persons. They need to know how to observe and actively listen, and then intervene.

We need to have training to develop our skills on the natural level and through spiritual formation (theological reflection) to appreciate the supernatural meaning of the event or intervention.

The Church requires a training regime for pastoral care. It needs to be open to everyone. We are all called to care for one another in Christ. It will have to be training that is didactic and which consists of active listening skills, obser vation techniques, and bereavement training. It will contain Christ-centered theology and will include a focus on theological reflection and teaching. It will reflect a traditional biblical view of biomedical ethics and moral decision making.

THE STANDARD CLINICAL MODEL OF PASTORAL CARE

Clinical Pastoral Education, (CPE has been the standard for training in the chaplaincy. I have four units of CPE which is about 1,600 hours of supervision and clinical patient visitation. Over the last twenty years, I have added many more hours in training and teaching. I have made countless patient visits and done crisis interventions. Unfortunately, I have found, for the most part, that the present CPE model is not compatible with the Christian view of pastoral care. My reasons for believing this are: CPE is not didactic enough, it does not teach or provide a formal training regime of observation and listening skills.

CPE tries to be all things to all people. As a result, the gospel message gets lost in cultural relativism. Many graduates of CPE programs, that I have interviewed, have tossed aside their Christian moorings. They have accepted a philosophy that is more Unitarian than Christian. Most seminaries and denominations require at least one Unit of CPE (400 hours) for ordination to ministry. It may be a major reason why many clergy today have wandered away from orthodox teaching on faith and morals. It tends to promote a relativistic pattern of acceptance that stresses inclusion and humanistic values. It espouses a belief that Jesus is not the way—He is *a* way. CPE teaches that to believe otherwise is to be a religious bigot and a fundamentalist ideologue. The CPE method throws you into the sea and says, "Let's talk about swimming. Did you like the water? How do you feel when the water is cold? Maybe you should try to rescue yourself sometime? What do you think?" CPE lacks a heart of a Jesus response. Theological reflection is a Christian discipline. It is focused on the work of the Holy Spirit and the love of Christ in the patient. CPE also lacks formal Christian teaching on biomedical ethics. In many places, it condones abortion, euthanasia, and sexual lifestyles and behavior that are contrary to biblical teaching and the Christian tradition. It often carries its relativistic pattern of theological nominalism into moral and ethical decision making. Finally, CPE is not open to everyone. If you want to take a unit of CPE training, you must have at least a bachelor's degree, or some acceptable equivalent.

THE BABY BOOMER GENERATION

The church is facing a great opportunity and challenge as the Baby Boomer Generation grows older and sicker. The size of this deluge is similar to, and feels like, the large number of persons who have illegally sought a better life in America. On both fronts we have been overwhelmed. The rising tide of the Baby Boomer Generation will likely swamp many institutions, hospitals, our government, and churches. Society and religion have been largely in denial about this huge wave of need that will crash upon our communities. Whether we like it or not, this tsunami will reach all of us. The church is not prepared, as it will need to be, to provide the pastoral care that will be required by this emerging ground swell. I am fifty-nine years old and I am coming close to retirement age. Behind me and ahead of me are many, more Baby Boomers.

The first thing we need to do in the midst of this storm, is for the whole church to become pastoral care platforms for God's Kingdom—the high ground of safety and care. I think we will see society less able to provide this support, and people will turn to quick fixes to relieve the pressure of this surging sea. Already some states have enacted laws that allow for doctor-assisted suicide. Limited medical resources and financial constraints will lead to rationing healthcare. The moral morass that much of the world is in will continue to support abortion on demand and a decline in the fabric of societal cohesion. America is in a free fall of debt, and although some have sounded the alarm, many are simply not paying attention to the words of warnings from these sentinels.

Pastoral care is the starting place for the church in the new millennium. It is the brides' glory to be the heart of His attention. "When, Lord, did we give you something to eat or drink? When did we welcome you as a stranger or give you clothes to wear or visit you while you were sick or in jail? The king will answer, "Whenever you did it for any of my people, no matter how unimportant they seemed, you did it for me" (Matt. 25:40ff cev). The desire to minister to the wounded comes from the heart of God's grace. It is cemented in our own story of pain and redemption, of being rescued and saved. Jesus is the bridegroom and where the king is, there is the kingdom. Below is a cognitive map that shows how our Pastoral Care Community is built.

THE PASTORAL CARE COMMUNITY

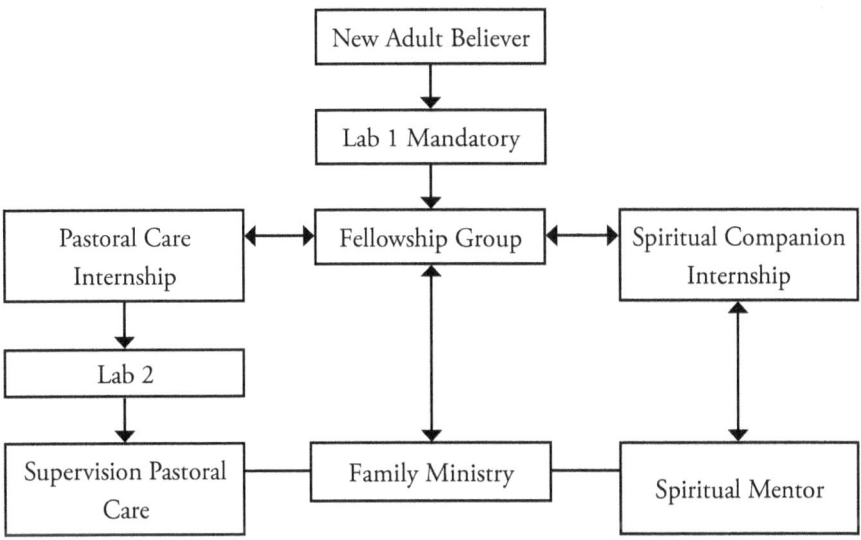

Pastoral Care Training is 100 hours per unit with supervision. Four hundred hours of training are required to graduate and be certified to provide pastoral care. Supervisor training consists of 1,200 hours of supervision along with taking Lab 2.

Family Ministry Training is for all adults who are parents or grandparents. It teaches how to make the family a church place. Sacraments, prayer, Christian education, and theological reflections are shared in the group.

The Spiritual Mentor Course is two years of training in the Spiritual Companion Ministry with weekly group meetings and discussion. It includes training to lead new groups.

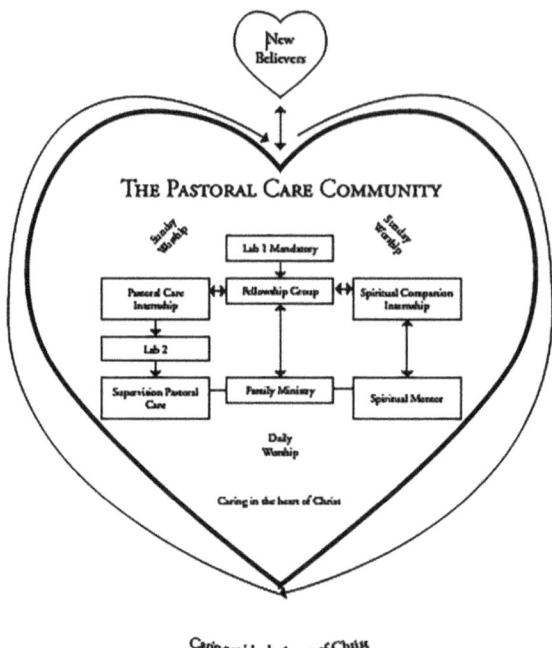

The Pastoral Care Community

Caring with the heart of Christ

THE METHODOLOGY OF THE PASTORAL CHURCH

The diagram describes the structures for training that we use in our Pastoral Care Heart-Centered Church. Lab 1 on active listening training is a mandatory requirement to join the congregation. The diagram is not static, but a living representation of how it works. Like the heart, the coronary arteries provide blood to keep the heart pumping. The training and mentoring feeds the pastoral care community. It helps us learn concrete listening skills and it helps us understand the reasons why people drop out of the church. It is a tool that focuses us on becoming a conscious community.

The Lab, developed by John Savage as his doctrinal dissertation, is the central element we use to build a common language and methodology for pastoral care formation.[95] Family training materials use the Bible and the Lectionary for readings on Sunday. We share teaching tools and outcomes in weekly fellowship groups. Parents are encouraged to share their experiences of teaching their children a spiritual formation in Christ. Internship is for those who desire to develop skills in visiting the sick, bereavement groups, and other pastoral care ministries. Spiritual Companions training is for those who are called to help others in their spiritual growth. We use the materials developed by Deacon Joseph Lessard and Karen Meyers. DVD's are viewed weekly and discussed by small groups for three years. These spiritual mentors need to have their own mentor and complete the course before they can mentor others. Being a supervisor begins with completing Lab 2 training to teach Lab 1 and 1,200 hours of supervised pastoral care work from the congregation. Pastoral Care Associates has been using this model for the last two years for training in providing pastoral care. The Priest or Deacon, in this model, is supervisor, trainer, and leader in worship. The priest models active listening skills and gives pastoral care to the people of God and oversees training and supervision. He supports emerging pastoral care ministries and defines the works and goals of the Church. He provides the vision and maintains the constant focus in the ministry of care. (See diagrams, "The Pastoral Care Community" and, "The Heart of Christ Model" on preceding pages.)

Caring with the heart of Christ is the active work of pastoral care ministry. It is the outward extension of caring for others. It is not enough just to care for others, but we must care for them as Christ cares for us. It is the intentional work of the church to engage the places of suffering, and the people there—hospitals, shelters, prisons, nursing homes, and care centers. It is to go and find places of ministry that are underserved and to take the caring love of Christ there.

Caring in the heart of Christ is the ongoing training and spiritual growth necessary to become a pastoral caregiver. Growth in the Spirit means a commitment to learning—not just education, but also experiential laboratory learning. Theological reflection and supervision are concrete ways we mature in the skills of caring in the heart of Christ. It is a commitment to a life of prayer, mentoring, and personal development. We need to learn from the heart of our Savior, to have the Savior's results. I am not talking about a short program with little or no labor. I am speaking of a life dedicated to caring for others. Some will say that it is too difficult to expect this from everyone. I don't expect this commitment from everyone; I expect it from those called by God and who are obedient to His calling. God is already seeding His church with a new awakening. The harvest is coming.[96] The question is this, is

He calling you? Here are three questions you might reflect on to see if God is calling you into His caring heart. Please write your reflections to the following questions:

Does caring for someone, maybe a sick friend or relative, make you feel close to God?

_____

_____

_____

_____

Have you heard your voice, when you have helped someone, sound like God's voice? Please write down what He is saying as you listen.

_____

_____

_____

_____

Have you seen yourself or others minister care to someone, and as you did pictured God's care for you? Please write down when you saw this picture.

_____

_____

_____

_____

RESOLUTION

The Harvest is over! A breath can be taken.
Left behind are the relics of another season.

        Containers lay empty in the dirt,
        Reminders of long days and hard work.

Well it's quiet now!
    A softer breeze blows in.
        Time to settle down
          And collect our strength again.

        The air is touched by sweetness,
        Giving tender caresses on the skin.
        And morning's resolution rests,
        Where trial and toil have been.

CHAPTER 8

SCRIPTURAL LEADERSHIP THAT CARES

I HAVE READ a lot of books that describe the role of a priest or minister and the virtues of the life of ministry and service. I know that books of this type are valuable and have their place in the tradition of the church. They tend, however, to reinforce the pattern and structure of the organizational church. The model that is most prevalent today in American culture sees the minister as a kind of religious CEO. He or she is saddled with the responsibilities of keeping the church buildings maintained, programs prospering, the church financially in the black, all the while keeping a growing and satisfied membership. I would like us to consider an alternative to this model that is centered on pastoral care and the caring side of leadership. If pastoral care is the heart of the Gospel, then leadership should draw us to it. Leadership and ministry should be patterned on the model that Jesus used and that the early church replicated and described in the Scriptures.

The prophet Isaiah describes the most succinctvision of leadership—one that shows us Jesus. Jesus is drawn to the suffering servant songs of the prophet in chapters 49-52. He begins his ministry in Luke's Gospel when He reads from the prophet Isaiah 61:1-2 He sees Himself as the "Son of Man," returning to Jerusalem like the people who rebuilt the temple after the Babylonian captivity.

Out of death and destruction, there is a promise and a resurrection. Jesus' pattern of ministry is to be that "Suffering Servant" who will redeem Israel and the whole world. What kind of leadership do we see in Jesus? The leadership for the kingdom of the new age requires a new type of king who leads by following, caring, shepherding, and by being vulnerable. We see the same pattern in the life of Saint Paul. Scriptural leadership is not a theological abstract role, or posture that emits power and success like the present institutional church model. Rather, it begins with the opposite idea of leadership. Out of weakness there is strength. Being first means being last and dying means to live. If you want to be rich become poor. If you want to be free become a slave to God. If you want to follow, be prepared to pick up your cross (see Mark 8:34-35).

I have been a priest for more than thirty years, and I have learned that believing the Scriptures about Jesus means, I had better be prepared to suffer. The biblical mantle of following, caring, shepherding, and vulnerability will always lead to a cross. It is a pattern that effects a certain outcome. If you want to be like Jesus, prepare to be treated like Him. If you want to lead like Jesus, prepare yourself for a journey to Jerusalem. I don't mean this in a fatalistic and depressed way. On the contrary, this way leads to eternal life. It is in direct contrast to the life that many clergy dream about. Many priests or ministers have a fantasy of a successful parish free from debt and growing by leaps and bounds. We have dreams of making more money to support the growing parish program. We search the parking lots and count the church attendance to validate or guilt ourselves on the virtues or failures of our vision of the church. Oh, I have been there in that space between the spaces—the in-between world of what we need to survive as a church, and what resources we really can count on. I have asked myself if this is really what the church has become. Must clergy always be wondering when the parish board will decide to reward or remove them? What is the real kind of biblical leadership that can challenge the cultural cheap imitation that is so unconscious and pervasive?

Biblical leadership begins with following: Jesus followed the will of the Father. He said that He would do what He saw the Father doing (see John 5:19-22). He picks twelve apostles to follow Him and in Luke He sends them out to rehearse leadership.[97] He teaches them with parables. They witness His miracles and His way of life.[98] They are introduced into a life of prayer.[99] They are brought into His heart of love and care because they followed Him.[100] Following Jesus means leaving behind the way the world thinks and its values. It means not just putting on a new set of ideas or learning a religious language or wearing a small piece of jewelry. It is a change of your whole life from following after fame, security, acceptance, or our ego to following Jesus and developing the same pattern inside your spirit that was built in the heart of Saint Paul and the apostles. Following is not mindless or irrational. It is based on faith. It is reasonable to come to believe. God is not a construct of the mind. He is not a higher power like electricity or magnetism. He is a personal experience of the heart.

Reason can get you to the door of belief, but following leads you inside God's house and to His Heart. It is impossible to come into the kingdom without following the king, and it is impossible to follow Him without faith. Every Christian leader knows when he or she started following. It wasn't because they were perfect or the best or the brightest. They experienced a conversion, and just like the apostles, Jesus knew them and called them anyway.[101] Stepping out into this calling requires faith. It begins with a willingness to risk the present and future and leave the past. It is a step that a person does not forget because it begins with possibilities, "Follow me and I will make you fishers of men,"[102] and from there it never ends. A leader who has given up on God's possibilities is not following and is in no position to lead. ("With God all things are possible.")[103] The calling can easily devolve into liturgical style over and against God's substance. The value of the tree is not in its shape, color, or leafy brilliance, but in its fruit. Hypocrisy is the appearance of leadership without the fruit of following. If the Pharisees had been following God, they would have accepted and led the people to Jesus.[104] They would have welcomed Him home and opened the doors of the Temple instead of laying plots in it to kill Him.[105]

My first parish had gone through a difficult transition of leadership before I got there. When I arrived, I was excited and ready for a new challenge. We had our first vestry meeting and after it was over, a prominent church member came up to me with a big smile and looked me straight in the eye and said, with a prideful tone, "We kill priests in this parish." It is a sad day when a parish learns the lessons of its power. I was reminded at that moment that following Jesus was not going to be a peaceful frolic in the park. It would require faithfulness and caring, without the assurance that things would work out or that the church would thrive. When the church begins to lead itself and does not follow, there is no limit to the damage it can do.

Jesus recognizes the importance of following the will of the Father. Without it, real leadership is not possible. It is not the only essential biblical principle He uses. Real leadership comes from caring and concern for the weak. In Luke 9:46 the apostles are arguing over who is the greatest. The argument is the same old worldly question of who knows best, and who is in charge. Jesus brings the power conflict to consciousness. He does not name a successor. He does not berate them for trying to take His job, or claiming their territory. He takes a child in His arms and breaks the attachment to power, ego, and vanity, by introducing the necessity of caring for the weakest little ones and protecting them. Biblical caring is produced by following Christ. We see caring for others throughout the New Testament and in the lives of the saints. Leadership that does not care seeks its own rewards. It divides and conquers and makes no excuses for its excesses. On the other hand, leadership that cares also serves. It welcomes new people, anticipates needs, and maintains humility through self disclosure. The three most deadly words in the world can be, "I don't care." A person can fill in the blanks after those three words. I don't care what you do or if you leave or if you need help or if I never see you again. The absence of caring kills relationships and wounds the church. Lord make my prayer," by God's grace, may I care for others and the world the way Christ cares for me."

Leadership that cares also guides. Shepherding is the pattern of the life of Jesus.[106] He is not without the necessary will to lead.

Christian leadership sets expectations and has boundaries in Christ. People who have a sense of belonging and participation want to be guided. Jesus is the Good Shepherd, but He is a shepherd and that job requires certain things. The job description includes: commitment, faithfulness, accountability, justice, and integrity. Paul was the leader of the communities he founded. He was not disengaged or aloof. He preached, guided, gave advice with hymns, sound reason, and insight into the Gospel. Leadership in Christ, shepherding does not mean that everything will just be great and that everyone will just agree with what the pastor says. It does mean that in times of disagreement or conflict, we are committed to working out the issues in an open and caring way. I have discovered that most of the conflicts that preoccupy the church are about the stuff we have: buildings, property, and maintenance. Or they are regarding decisions about the aesthetic appearances of the interior of the church and the needed funds to support the staff and parish programs. I am not aware that Paul in any of his letters is concerned with stuff. He is concerned about the financial necessities for saints who are experiencing hardships. Not once does he write about the latest church renovation or expansion of the church gym. Not once does he describe how the altar looked or which direction it should face east or west or if it should have an altar rail or not. Paul always stays focused on the teachings of the Gospel. Christian leadership does not lose sight of the heart of the gospel by being overly concerned about the material stuff. I do suppose that we have to talk about the stuff once in awhile, but not at the expense of the Gospel and not to the degree we often do. I have discussed the need for shepherds who care for the sheep. They don't place a higher value on the church stuff at the expense of having a caring ministry.

God calls Christian leaders into a relationship that requires vulnerability. Leadership in Christ includes being vulnerable to my weaknesses. Sharing our insecurities and difficulties is healthy. Saint Paul often communicated his needs, disappointments, conflicts, and pain with the churches he founded. In both letters to the Corinthians,[107] Paul confronts those who oppose him and in the process, provides a lot of selfdisclosure. Christian leadership does not hide behind the cloak of a ministerial role, but is open about personal shortcomings and accepts the limitations of others. All Paul's letters have the quality of being written by a real person who is dealing with his own calling and its application.[108] Over and over again he tells the story of his sinful intent to persecute the Church and his conversion to following Christ.[109] Jesus shows us His vulnerability throughout the gospels. When His friend Lazarus dies, he weeps. When He speaks about His own death on the cross, he is sorrowful. When He is frustrated by the peoples' lack of faith or by their demands for signs, he is impatient.[110] In fact we can say that the New Testament shows God's vulnerability to all of us.

AUTHORITY IN CHRIST

What is the proper place of authority and its importance in the Body of Christ? The place to start is the place where the values of following, caring, shepherding, and vulnerability are first lived out. We practice leadership with the people we love. Families are the primary residence of the Holy Spirit. We experience the benefits of security and belonging when familial relationships are centered in Christ. The pattern of authority begins and is taught in the framework of the family. Parents love and care for their children by training them. Parental authority that is caring will help children grow up into disciples of Christ. We see this kind of metaphor in Saint Paul's writings to the communities he founded when he refers to himself as a spiritual father (see 1 Thess. 2:11). He does not use his authority in Christ to dominate, but to mirror the nature of Christ's leadership. It was the love of the Father that produced the incarnation. Paul sees this caring as the soul of his own ministry of building up the kingdom of God. Authority that is oppressive or controlling robs the church of its witness of caring in Christ. It produces the fruit of conflict and jealousy within the church. In contrast, the value of caring leadership and ordination is that it extends the ministry outward to evangelize the world. Christian leadership provides a point of unity in teaching and training. It is effective when it is seen, heard, and lived with Christ's heart.

Our culture often understands authority as power over a person or a group of persons. Power can be used as a substitute for caring. In the absence of love, people settle for power. The trade off of power for love leads to abuse. Jesus models love and caring as the heart of the pattern of God's kingdom. New Testament authority shepherds the sheep from behind by persuading, encouraging, guiding, obser ving, and communicating training and teaching. The church uses its moral and spiritual authority to set moral and religious boundaries in keeping with biblical teaching to provide safety for the sheep. When Jesus is confronted with the use of His authority to protect Himself, He moves away from it and replaces it with caring. The Beatitudes are an example (see Matt. 5:1-12). People of His day recognized that He had authority that was different from that of the Pharisees. He didn't need to engineer His authority or spin it to control anyone. Jesus counsels with the Father to make decisions. Sometimes He includes the apostles. We clearly see, however, that His authority to make decisions is based on His obedience to the will of the Father.

I have been to a lot of vestry meetings and I have often wondered why, after we have said a prayer, decisions becomes the domain of the membership. Biblical principles are often put aside or forgotten when we get down to the business of running the church. The church is not our possession. It is not a thing or a private club or some unchangeable static entity. The church without the authority of caring is a dreadful business.

I certainly accept the need for a hierarchy. Church history is full of evidence all the way back to Saint Paul and the apostles of the importance of structured leadership. All denominations have a system of leadership and authority. The importance of grounding its use in a caring way does not diminish the need for boundaries and discipline, but rather places its content and purpose in the Christ's heart of caring.

THE PASTORAL CARE MODEL OF SPIRITUAL COMMUNITY

Our model sees the responsibility of parents and grandparents to raise our children in the faith. The clergy assists them in this most important work of pastoral care. Training within the broader church is for adults. Children are trained and taught the faith by the parents in the family by their example and teaching. I know that this idea is not the norm. However we need to develop a Church life that intentionally ministers to the dropped out person. I can safely say from my years in pastoral care, and thousands of interviews that roughly eighty percent of the people I see in the hospital have little or no connection to the institutional church.

I know that the institutional model works for about twenty percent of the people. The members who are active—attend at least two times a month and regularly contribute—are a small number compared to the dropped-out or un-churched. Twenty percent of the population is happy with the present institutional model. The vast majority of lapsed Christians may need a pastoral care-centered community to experience Jesus Christ and become His disciples. I believe that now is the time to build pastoral communities using a caring framework. The vast majority of lapsed Christians have little or no connection to the institutional church, and are unlikely to develop one. Building new churches in the old ways just tends to further subdivide a dwindling supply of active members. We have an opportunity to do something different. We have a divine invitation to build up pastoral caregivers to counter the inroads of our pervasive materialistic culture. I am not interested in the traditional planting of churches, but in training people in God's service. A church building has never been taken up to heaven. The Scriptures say that a heavenly temple awaits us, and that a place is prepared for us. The Holy Jerusalem is being built not with bricks and mortar, but with our lives. We are the living stones, a building not built by hands but by love and caring, in the Heart of God.[111] Jesus is the cornerstone which cements together every good work.

Building a pastoral care community depends on important gifts of the Spirit. It will require the leadership to be diligent and observant to maintain the qualities of following, caring, guiding, and vulnerability. It will have to be disciplined and attuned to reframe congregational life in a different pattern that contrasts the culture's fascination with immediacy and entertainment. Values of patience and trust will have to be central virtues for formation and training. It will require time and consistent participation to mature and grow. Most importantly, it will require self-denial.

Our culture is absolutely opposed to the idea of delaying anything or being inconvenienced. Yet, Jesus invited those who followed him to put aside their own agenda and adopt His. "Let the dead bury their dead" (Matt. 8:22 cev), means, "Don't let anything come between you and following me." We see large and small churches competing with the culture to maintain active members. The institutional church clamors for the attention of its members in a smaller and smaller window of free time. The demands of our modern culture can deprive our children of their faith. Our culture rewards and expects performance in soccer, dance, or a million other quasi-essential pastimes. Caring for one another in Christ is not one of them.

An ex college student of mine called me sometime ago and said how much he had enjoyed the class I taught him on active listening. The course was taught using the Lead Plus materials developed by John Savage. He told me that he had graduated and was now in charge of a men's ministry at one of the largest congregations in Phoenix. He asked me if I would teach the class to some of the men in the group. I reminded him that the class was forty hours long and took four weekends to complete. He felt sure that he could get together a large group. We discussed where to offer the lab and when dates could be arranged. Well, as time went on and I had not heard from him, I called him. He then told me that only a few men had decided to attend. I said okay we will add those to some other people who would like to take the lab and we could have a small group. Guess how many finally decided to attend from that church? Exactly zero, not one could free up his or her calendar for such a long training.

Matthew 22:14 says, "Many are called, but few are chosen" (nrsv). I have seen the truth of this statement over and over again. Jesus is preparing us to realize that only a few will respond to His invitation. We need to get used to the idea that we are going to be working with small groups. It's as if the Lord wants us to know that the pastoral care model works best with two or three or six or eight. Don't expect crowds. Prepare for only a few attendees at a time. Pastoral leadership is not about getting the biggest bang for your buck. It is about acting in accord with God's care plan and doing things His way.

GOD'S CARE PLAN FOR MY LIFE/ THE LIFE OF THE CHURCH

Every admission into the hospital creates a care plan. The plan includes tests, treatments, results, medications, and plans for discharge. It is a very structured set of criteria that benefits the patient. It describes the requirements for discharge either for further treatment or for release home. Without a discharge plan, the hospital would not know when it was medically safe to release a patient.

I think God has a care plan for each one of us. He has put the plan in motion by giving us the Holy Spirit. The person of Jesus is the criteria for our life in God's love. We look into His life of caring and we see and experience what God's plan looks like. God has a treatment plan at work in my life and yours. His healing grace leads us into a deeper trust and love for Him. His sweet Spirit consoles and strengthens us with His divine therapy (see John 14:15-22). No matter where we have come from; no matter how wounded or hurt we have been; no matter how much pain or failure we have endured; no matter what sin we have committed, God's care plan for you and me can and will overcome all (see Rom. 8:37-39).

Here are some thoughts that may help you realize God's plan for your life:

Please write a short reflection from your recent experiences of hardships or sufferings.

_____

_____

_____

_____

Write a short list of things you have learned from the above experience.

_____

_____

_____

_____

Please identify for yourself anything in your life that needs to change.

_____

_____

_____

_____

From the things examined above, is there anyone with whom you need to share the benefits of God's Care plan? Please write their names below and list the gifts of care they need from you.

_____

_____

_____

_____

Final Thoughts

Straight from a Pastors Heart—A Systematic *Theology of Pastoral Care*

Volume

I HOPE YOU have enjoyed volume one. The task ahead is going require a larger work than just one book. I have endeavored in this first volume to translate for you some of the ways God has been involved in my life. It is a living theological work in progress. I hope you have gotten some insight into God's care and love for you. It is my prayer that you will grow in love by reading and reflecting on what you have heard, seen, and felt by sharing my experience of pastoral care ministry. It is important at this time and with the stresses Christians are under to examine the direction that the Holy Spirit is leading us. I trust that my words and experiences have been an encouragement to you in your journey with Christ.

I especially thank our chaplains and our board of directors of Pastoral Care Associates for their support in writing this book. Most importantly, is the support of my wife, Dorothy, and in our community Sister Margaret LaPenna and our family and friends who have encouraged me to write and have prayed for me to make this work a reality.

In the Holy name of Jesus
The Rev. Michael Lessard

NOTES

1. Luke 10:5-6; Matt. 10:13.

2. Matt. 4:1ff; Mark 1:13ff, Luke 4:2ff.

3. Mark 8:31-32; Matt. 16:21-24.

4. Isa. 53:1-13.

5. See Bibliography 'Paul Tillich'

6. Rom. 8:34-35—A sign of Jesus' caring is intercession; prayer for us.

7. 1 Cor. 15:53—A quick moment from life to life.

8. John 10:11-14—Jesus cares and as a good shepherd risks His life for us.

9. Ps. 23:3-5—He is the Good Shepherd and He provides safety by following Him.

10. Ps. 23:4 (nrsv)—The good shepherd has boundaries.

11. "Culture of Death," Encyclical Letter; Pope John Paul 11

12. John 15:1–12—Abiding in Christ's love and care. (nrsv translation)

13. Gen. 2:15-17—To till and keep the Garden.

14. Gen. 3:15-16—God gives, "a promise" of an offspring to

15. strike at the enemies head.

16. Gen. 3:20-22—God made clothes for Adam and Eve.

17. Rom. 8:18-26—In Christ we receive freedom as the children of God.

18. Gen. 4:9 (nrsv)—Do I care where my brother may be?

19. Lev. 14:10-21; Acts 2:10, 17;—Oil for priestly prescriptions for healing and atonement.

20. Rom. 8:16—We are children of God in His Spirit.

21. Mark 6:34 (nrsv); Matt. 9:36.

22. Rom. 8:9-11—The Holy Spirit gives us the life of the resurrection.

23. *Book of Common Prayer*, Catholic Sacramentary.

24. John 16:1-15—The Holy Spirit will counsel and guide Apostles.

25. John 2:1-11—The wedding in Cana.

26. Matt. 5:1-11; Mark 5:33-43; Luke 10:17-34;. John 1:35-51.

27. *Leadership, Education, and Development Lab 1* training manual—LEAD PLUS (see bibliography).

28. Gal. 3:23-4:8—Baptized as heirs, God's children.

29. Isa. 28:14ff; 1 Cor. 15:50-58—Covenant with death is enjoy ourselves today, tomorrow we may die; God sets a precious new cornerstone, a man who opposes this covenant with death.

30. Luke 1:46-48—Magnify the Lord, Mary's prophetic word and our call in the Spirit.

31. Eph. 1:3—We are given every spiritual blessing.

32. John 15:1-12—Abiding with Jesus means to abide with God the Father.

33. Luke 23:34 (nrsv)

34. Matt. 6-15; Luke 7:47-48; Eph. 4:32—Forgiveness is donated and received.

35. Catholic absolution prayer and absolution in the *Book of Common Prayer* (see bibliography).

36. Eph. 2:15-22—Peace is given by Christ to the believer.

37. John 20:19-21 (nrsv) Some translations say: "Greetings" The peace that Jesus gives is from the person of God's Sabbath rest.

38. Matt. 28:16-20

39. Matt. 4:23-24, 9:35; Mark 1:34; Luke 4:40.

40. *Healing* (see bibliography).

41. *Getting the Love You Want* (see bibliography).

42. LEAD PLUS (see bibliography Student Manual) 42. *Getting the Love You Want* (see bibliography).

43. John 21:15-18 (nrsv)—Feeding the Church from salvation and forgiveness.

44. Acts 9:1-9; 1 Cor. 15:9; Gal. 1:13—Paul's proclamation.

45. Luke 24:36—Jesus gives peace through the Resurrection. (nrsv)

46. John 2:1-11—A wedding at Cana.

47. Luke 7:36-50—Jesus is anointed by a repentant woman.

48. *Book of Common Prayer* (see bibliography), Liturgy of Baptism.

49. *Iron John* (see bibliography), by Robert Bly.

50. Mark 1:29-34—The first miracle in the Gospel of Mark is to Simon's mother-in-law.

51. Luke 9:18; John 6:15—Jesus spent time alone praying.

52. 2 Chron. 2:4; 13:11; 26:16; Ps. 141:2; Rev. 8:4—incense goes up to God's altar.

53. 1 Sam. 3:10ff—Samuel is called by God to be a prophet.

54. Matt. 10:27; 11:15; 13:9; Mark 4:9; Luke 8:8 (nrsv)— hearing God's Word with open ears.

55. Matt. 8:5-13; 15:21-28—Jesus finds faith in unusual people.

56. Matt. 6:9-13; Luke 11:2-5—Our Father

57. John 11:17-44—Lazarus brought to life.

58. Rom. 8:27-35; Heb. 7:22-28—He intercedes for us to God the Father.

59. 1 Cor. 12:1-11—The Spiritual Gifts.

60. Luke 4:16-23—Jesus affirms His calling to redeem Israel.

61. John 3:1-19—The Spirit of God brings new life and freedom from fear.

62. Mark 7:31-36; 10:13-16; Luke 5:12-15; 8:44-47.

63. Matt. 7:16-20; John 15:2-16—Fruit that is good and is abiding in the vine.

64. Mark 8:22-25; John 9:1-41—Healing the blind let's us see Jesus.

65. John 13:1-12—Washing the apostles feet is a sign of caring

66. Matt. 8:1-10; Luke 7:11-17-Two examples of Jesus caring for people around Him.

67. John 20:24-29—Jesus invites Thomas to experience redemption, seeing, hearing and feelings.

68. "The Three Ages of the Interior Life," (see bibliography).

69. John 12: 37-41—Hardened hearts resist grace.

70. Gen. 2:2-4—God's rest ends creation and begins re-creation of humanity. Exod. 16:23-29; Lev. 23:1-3— Gives the prescription of the law and Old Testament covenant.

71. Matt. 12:1-14—Jesus teaches about the Sabbath. Luke 14:1-5p; John 5:1-18—Jesus heals on the Sabbath.

72. Exod. 32:22-25—It is amazing how idols are quickly and magically created.

73. Matt. 4:1ff; Mark 1:13ff; Luke 4:2ff—The Temptations of Christ.

74. John 19:34-36—The blood shed for sin and the waters of humanities re-birth.

75. "Cognitive Map of Linguistic System," adapted from *LEAD PLUS* Student Training Manual (see bibliography).

76. John 4:9-15—Jesus is the Living Water.

77. Matt. 21:18-20; Mark 11:13-14, 20-24—Jesus expects us to produce fruit.

78. John 17:22-26—Unity among the brethren mirrors the unity between Christ and the Father.

79. Matt. 3:13-17; Mark 1:9-11; Luke 3:21-22 (nrsv)—The Fathers word of affirmation to Jesus.

80. Mark 1:9-11 (nrsv)—We are called by the same affirmation in Christ.

81. Rev. 21:1-27—The new Jerusalem—heaven's domain.

82. Rom. 1:7; 1 Cor. 1:2-3; 2 Cor. 1:1; Phil. 1:1-2 (nrsv)— Paul affirms his churches.

83. Luke 11:37-53; John 14:23-24—Keeping and producing God's Word in Christ.

84. Mark 10:17-29; John 3:1-19—The rich young man and Nicodemus are examples that Jesus' invitation comes with a choice.

85. Rom. 8:35-38 (cev)—Nothing can separate us from the love of God.

86. Matt. 13:45—Kingdom of God is like a pearl of great price.

87. John 4:13-38—Samaritan woman experiences Christ's care.

88. Mark 4:21-23 (nrsv)—Don't hide your light.

89. John 1:3-13; 9:36-40—Jesus is the light of the world.

90. Mark 9:14-29.

91. Mark 12:41-44; Luke 21:1-4.

92. John 8:1-11—The woman caught in adultery.

93. Matt. 8:28-34; Mark 5:1-20; Luke 8:26-36

94. Matt. 8:23-27; Mark 4:35-41; Luke 8:22-25; John 6:1521—Jesus rescues the Apostles from the fury of the sea

95. *The Bored and Apathetic Church Member* (see bibliography).

96. John 5:19-22 Jesus Mirrors the Fathers communication.

97. Luke 10:1-17.

98. Matt. 4:19-22; Mark 1:16-20; Luke 5:1-11.

99. Matt. 6:5-14; Luke 11:2-4—Jesus models prayer that is not a performance.

100. Matt. 13:10-16, Mark 4:10-11, Luke 8:9-10 Jesus introduces us into a life of prayer.

101. Matt. 4:20; Mark 1:18; Luke 5:11ff; John 1:37—Following Jesus is a decision.

102. Matt. 4:18-22—Jesus Calls the Apostles to follow and prepare for a catch of people into God's kingdom.

103. Matt. 19:26; Mark 9:23—The possibilities are endless with God's love.

104. John 9:35-41—The blindness of those entrusted to lead the people cannot see Jesus.

105. John 11:45-55—Plots to eliminate God's Word for the sake of man's word.

106. John 10:1-21—Jesus is the Good Shepherd who gives His life for the sheep.

107. 1 Cor. 1:10-17; 2 Cor. 10-11—Paul's vulnerability.

108. Rom. 7:7-18—Sin is at work but grace abounds.

109. Gal. 1:13ff; 1 Cor. 15:9ff; Phil. 3:1-10.

110. John 4:48ff; Matt. 16:4ff—Wanting signs and wonders, but not belief.

111. Rev.11:1-19.15:5-8—God's temple is in our hearts, the love of Christ.

BIBLIOGRAPHY FOR
STRAIGHT FROM THE HEART

Already Gone, by Ham, Ken and Beemer, Britt, Master Books, 2009

Encyclical Letter, Evangelium Vitae, Pope John Paul II, On the Value and Inviolability of Human Life, March 25,1995

Getting the Love You Want, by Hendrix, Harville, Henry Holt and Co. Updated edition, Dec. 26, 2007

Guilt and Grace, by Tournier, Paul, Hudder. Stoughton Ltd. January 1, 1974

Healing, by MacNutt, Francis, Bantam, 1983

Holy Bible, Contemporary English Version, American Bible Society, 1995

Iron John, by Bly, Robert, Addison-Wesley, 1990

Lab 1 Student Manual, Learning the Language of Healing, LEAD PLUS
Lab 1 Trainers Manual, LEAD PLUS, pg. 58, Neuro-Linguistic Programming

Loving and Curing the Neurotic, by Terruwe, Anna and Baars, Conrad, Arlington House 1972.*Poverty of Spirit* by Metz, Johannes Baptist, copyright 1968, 1998; by the Missionary Society of Saint Paul the Apostle, in the state of New York.

The Book of Common Prayer 1978, Oxford University Press.

The Bored and Apathetic Church Member, by Savage, John, LEAD PLUS

The Cost of Discipleship, by Bonheoffer, Dietrich, Macmillan, 1959

The Courage to Be, by Tillich, Paul, Yale University Press, 1952

The Holy Bible, New Revised Standard Version, Oxford University Press, Copyright 1989

The Jerome Biblical Commentary, Prentice Hall Inc. 1968

The Meaning of Person, by Tournier, Paul, Copyright 1957, Published with arrangements, Harper Collins Publisher

The Road Less Traveled, by Peck, M. Scott, Simon and Shuster, 1978
The Three Ages of the Interior Life, by Lagrange, Reginald, Garrigou, Saint Benedicts Press, Tan Books. Vol. 1 and Vol.2

The Way of Perfection, by Avila, Saint Theresa, Edger Allison Peers, 1999, Copyright 1946, 1977, by Reed and Ward LTD, first published in 1944.

Theological Anthropology, by Von Balthazar, Hans Urs, Sheed and Ward, New York, 1967

We Dare to Say Our Father, by Everly, Louis, Doubleday, 1975

Young's Analytical Concordance to the Bible, Young, Robert, WM. B. Eerdmans Publishing Company 1964, reprinted 1976

www.ingramcontent.com/pod-product-compliance
Lightning Source LLC
Chambersburg PA
CBHW051215120626
46547CB00013B/1363